❧ Can You See Me Naked? ❧

Grow in a Conscious Relationship

Can You See Me Naked?

Grow in a Conscious Relationship

Written for Men by a Woman

Adelé Green
ACMC, N.Dip. PR, Dip IH, NLP, PSI³

Published by Life Philosophy
PO Box 412714, Craighall, Johannesburg,
South Africa, 2024
www.lifephilosophy.co.za
adele@lifephilosophy.co.za

Available from:
www.nakedwithadele.com
Selected bookstores

Second edition 2013

Can you see me naked? Grow in a conscious relationship
ISBN 978-0-620-57385-6

Copyright © 2013 Adelé Green

This publication enjoys copyright under the Berne Convention. In terms of the Copyright Act, No. 98 of 1978, no part of this publication may be reproduced, stored in a retrieval system, or transmitted, in any form or by any means, without the prior written permission of the publisher. A catalogue copy of this book is available in the South African National Library.

Edited by Victoria Smith
Proofread by Bunty Cope
Cover design by Justin B. Rens
Back jacket blurb by Matthew Doyle
Printed by Lightningsource, London, United Kingdom

Acknowledgements:
Oriah Mountain Dreamer, "The Dance" © 2001.
Published by HarperONE, San Francisco. All rights reserved.
Quote presented with permission of the author.
www.oriah.org

May this book serve you when you feel stuck in your relationship; not on how to act, but by enabling you to stop and reflect on what you understand and observe, both inside and outside your own needs. I wrote it through learning painful but vulnerable lessons during my three marriages, and trusting in the guidance of my dreams.

In gratitude, I dedicate this book to all the men in my life: fathers, guardians, lovers, husbands, sons and intimate male friends. I love you all for your gifts of insight as I got to know myself better. And my gratitude also extends to God's male side, if there is one, for humouring my expectations about the Perfect Man. I projected my rejected inner masculine aspects onto the men in my world and blamed them for what I couldn't take responsibility for myself. This book is the end product – for the benefit of many evolving women and to bring their male partners a small vestige of understanding of what makes women tick.

Purpose Of This Book

Ever since Eve first demystified Adam, men have been baffled by the vagaries of women. I wrote this book in the hope that I might help men understand, or at least unravel, some of the complexities of the opposite sex and assist women in their emotional development and evolution at the same time. Hopefully, this will improve their personal relationships. The book aims to give men more insight into their relationships with their female partners and advises them on dealing with and managing expectations. It is written from the feminine perspective and offers women a better understanding of how their behaviour can shape or influence the success or failure of their personal partnerships.

Foreword

I was pleasantly surprised when Adelé told me she was writing a book about women for men.

My response was to add comments and explain to her that no matter how entertaining the read, the book did not assist in breaking old paradigms of belief. After the first read I was able to understand that my own view here might be the very obstacle to what is truly a thought-provoking experience. It stands alone. To all this she had no response and just smiled (the female response).

Then I reread the book, this time putting myself in a woman's role and I had a different response altogether. I was surprised at how emotional women really are.

From a male, logical perspective there is a compelling reason for understanding this book. The book reaffirms the natural order of the universe, which men and women need to learn to understand and articulate.

Choosing the path of the natural order of things is what allows nature to flow, as it recognises the support of the opposite forces and becomes self-supportive. In my opinion, men have yet to understand this principle fully.

The big question is: will we be bold and brave enough to support, understand and allow full expression of that which appears to us as the opposite?

Adelé has reached out to men, and exposed the feminine. The choice men face is to be supportive or non-supportive. Will we men be able to make ourselves equal in the same way? I tested one of her hypotheses about gazing lovingly at women and had a few over-the-shoulder return glances. Recognising each other…this is the engagement that this book challenges us with.

Colin Byrne
Philosopher and Friend

Table Of Contents

Introduction	14
Setting the Stage	19

PART ONE
Introducing the Conscious Relationship Foundation 23

1	Can Insecure Men Open Women's Hearts?	25
2	Projecting Into The Mirror	31
3	How Do I Know It Is Love?	37
4	Is She The One?	51
5	Am I Ready For This Kind Of Commitment?	61
6	What Is Codependence And How Do I Avoid It?	71

PART TWO
Understanding How Conscious Relationships Work 77

7	Whose Stuff Is This Anyway?	79
8	Will I Ever Break Through This?	91
9	What If I'm Not Good Enough?	113
10	Feeling Alone Inside The Relationship	121

11	The Impact of Attachment	131
12	Too Close for Comfort	141
13	How Do I Maintain My Freedom?	151
14	Free Love	159

PART THREE
Understanding What Is behind Her Triggers 171

15	What Is This Constant Need for Appreciation?	173
16	What Does It Mean When She Says That She Doesn't Feel Seen and Heard?	185
17	Fly Dragon Fly – Her Dragonfly Transformation	193
18	The Shadow Side of Her Basic Needs	203
19	Finding Herself	221

PART FOUR
What You Can Do to Assist Her Transformation 237

20	How Can She Be Taught to Nurture Herself?	239
21	Learning Consciously through Conflict	253
22	Developing Feminine Leadership Skills	261
23	What Happened to Intimacy and Sensual Expression?	267
24	Did You See Me Naked?	285

Conclusion	291
Recommended Reading & Bibliography	296
Index	297
Author Biography	302

Introduction

You probably picked up this book because you've reached a point in your relationship where you don't feel you can make your partner happy. Has she withdrawn from you? Are you trying to bring her closer and repair the relationship between you?

Before you can understand the tools offered here, you'll be taken on a journey through the *transformation of women*. Written from the heart of a woman, revealing inner struggles from a feminine perspective, it serves one purpose – to invite you to see, hear and feel the world from your partner's viewpoint.

What you can expect is to grow beyond your own beliefs and values in a more conscious way. This is a process book that reads like a story, and with each read you'll gain deeper insights than you had before. Although you'll be offered information and tools, the best solution is to discover your own perspective as your knowledge grows. Empower your need to lead as the masculine in your relationship.

For the woman in your life, it offers an expression of language and different perspectives that resonate with her inner transformation, helping her to emerge as the new feminine. She will be able to contribute to her relationship consciously and positively, rather than withdraw or destroy the life she has built just because she feels misunderstood.

A woman is often not aware that what she blames a man for is the reflection he sends back to her about her own relationship with herself. Often women seem unwilling to act on their own needs, apart from talking about them, and this book will help with that. A conscious relationship has the potential to be a shared journey towards greater intimacy ... the one thing every woman wants deep inside, but is too scared to admit, even to herself.

Together we will delve into the relationship questions you might already be asking. This book provides perspectives that help women to acknowledge and value themselves, as well as tools for you that help with mirroring, validating and empathising. As her man, you have the power *to plant the seeds that will allow her to open up again*, to be as radiant as she was when you first met her and fell in love with her.

The book will be presented in four parts:
- Part 1 introduces the foundation of conscious relationships as expressed through ideas, boundaries, expectations and values. It will challenge you to review what you already believe. You might change your current interactions as you learn. Expect emotions to surface as you agree or disagree with my theories! Take note, especially, of any resistance you may be feeling towards those ideas, including your level of sensitivity to the feminine viewpoint.
- Part 2 discusses the polarities of male and female development in a relationship. You may already be asking questions like "Whose stuff is it anyway?" "Will I ever break through this?" "Why am I feeling alone in this relationship?" or "What if I am not good enough?"

❀ For women Part 3 reveals the inner intuitive language of the feminine *journey* that a woman experiences as the hidden pain in the dark corner of her heart. This influences her choice about which parts of herself she brings into the relationship. For you, her partner, it helps to create an understanding of the seemingly illogical behaviour you sometimes observe in the relationship – behaviour that probably drives you crazy. In this, the most challenging part of the book, I invite you to dig deeper into the spiritual nature of the women in your life: What do her emotions mask? What life lessons are being presented to her? What happens in her inner world when she withdraws?

❀ Part 4 provides practical guidance on how a woman can and should develop four essential skills – nurturing, leadership, intimacy and the ability to deal with conflict – as well as ways in which you can support her in this. Mastering these qualities will result in her becoming more available to you. If part three is about what lies below the iceberg, part four reveals what is on the surface.

Collectively, feminine evolution draws on trusting the inner wisdom of women. Transformation is necessary for the next stage of development as a female collective. Women will develop wisdom, even under cover if society remains ignorant of the natural evolution of the feminine in the final stage. What doesn't work in your relationship happens because of a destructive and misunderstood energy that covertly influences women and subconsciously controls their behaviour.

People have always been afraid of what they don't understand. A woman will leave a man, her family and her community if she needs to, in order to experience this part of her evolution, without necessarily understanding why or being able to explain it to anyone. I looked everywhere to find a way to understand what was happening to me. Once I understood, I wanted to make it easier for other women to understand and heal. I have found books written especially for men to understand men, and books written by men about women, but women choose poetry and creative writing to reveal their souls – mediums that are difficult for men to understand.

It is my vision that women will *move on from feeling that their boundaries are being violated*, to expressing what they need in their relationships with the clear intention of creating equality within those relationships. Your partner may be playing victim games with you to get what she wants, or controlling you subconsciously with hidden blame for her past pain, in an effort to protect herself. The natural essence of womankind is open, authentic and embracing. It has a softness that is kind and gentle. When pure, it can heal in a way that no other emotion can. However, when a woman feels misunderstood or unheard, it's simply too difficult to be soft and embracing. How strange, then, that I ask her man to reach into his feminine side to give space for his partner to heal. Yet here you are, reading these words. Whatever you decide to do, I want you to know that writing this book was my healing process. Learning how to express clearly what I need, and opening myself up to receive it, changed the nature of my relationship. I hope it will do the same for you.

Yes, this is about meeting the unmet needs of women, and if men could solve this common problem, everyone would be far happier. As you read through this book, you will discover – and even be surprised by – your blind spots. Be warned: as awareness opens your mind, you will need compassion, not only for your partner, but for yourself as well. Allow time to do what time does. How can a man love a woman if he doesn't yet know how to love himself?

My wish is that she will be intrigued by your conversations and read this book too. No doubt she will wonder what a man can know about her needs that she doesn't.

You might be disappointed if you're expecting a book that introduces what conscious relationships are. This book offers a process that is designed to help you discover more about yourself through your relationship as well as information. I hope it starts a pillow fight in your heart because the most important legacy you will ever leave is the collection of memories in your partner's mind. By the time you finish this book, you will understand why you aren't making her happy and what you can do about it. But I'm getting ahead of myself...

Setting The Stage

∼Awareness is a lonely and imagined form. Gazing into space, one is aware of amorphous details. And, as you observe, a shape forms. Awareness is the ultimate masculine, and matter the ultimate feminine abstract. As they unite for the first time, the first moment of intimacy occurs. Magically, spirit is infused into existence as matter feels itself to be observed and known, and with this reaction the world is complete. ∼

Living consciously is a decision, a choice to bring fresh eyes to what we observe without applying our past experiences and beliefs.

Relating to each other is awareness experiencing itself. We feel alive as we see ourselves through our relationships. Both male and female aspects connect intimately to experience the wholeness of the self through the other.

The capacity to experience intimacy between the masculine and the feminine depends on our understanding of the boundaries we use to define our image of ourselves. At one end, the soul craves to rise up, to be free of all boundaries and, at the same time, the body needs boundaries to protect its identity. An open heart craves to connect intimately in order to be acknowledged by conscious awareness to experience its wholeness. In relationships, boundaries are pushed by the masculine in the guise of freedom. But pain cuts the connection with the soul and builds walls in a relationship; walls that bring safety, and with it, separation. Boundaries are very necessary if we are to heal and they need to be respected in relationships. It's a case of "where angels fear to tread". We are not sure of the impact of setting boundaries, so we fear going there. We conclude that the soul needs no boundaries but on the other end of the spectrum, our pain requires many boundaries.

The tendency of the masculine is to gaze toward the feminine, to which she is receptive. This activates their desire for closeness and the potential for intimacy. Like a seed that is planted, what encourages it to grow? What creates a fertile environment? In relationships, the potential levels on which to connect are the physical, emotional, intellectual and spiritual. What supports the connection are the necessary boundaries that honour the potential of the connection. Both elusive and real, boundaries give sense and safety to the mind, which then becomes the fertile soil for growth.

When a woman feels threatened or vulnerable by a man's appreciation of her beauty, her shadow emerges, indicating that it's time for her to speak up about her real, unaddressed needs. It is this failure to address the real and unhealed issues that results in the violation of the feminine, sometimes through rape and abuse.

Her soul craves the intimacy that transforms her through the dance between the masculine and the feminine. This book is intended for the dialogue your masculine shadow will invoke, as you engage to support your female partner during her inner struggle. As she gives the emerging feminine a voice, she invites you to speak, with your gaze, for the emerging masculine. But she needs your greatest respect for her vulnerability.

The feminine cannot exist on its own; it can only exist in relation to the masculine. I sincerely hope that this book will encourage the masculine voice to reveal itself, as it too shines light on its shadow.

Sometimes authors like to tell readers how to read their books. This book has a special note of *reader beware:* your understanding will increase, as the information builds in your subconscious, each time you read it over time – meaning that what you think you understand the first time around may change the next time you read it.

PART ONE

Introducing the

Conscious Relationship Foundation

Chapter 1

❦I recognize my ego

When I do not give freely

When fear of rejection

Teaches me about unconditional love

It is my past experience

That creates the illusion of fear

But in reality

It has no power in the moment ❦

– The Limits of My Love

Can Insecure Men Open Women's Hearts?

When we connect with, engage, and participate fully in the world, we cannot afford to be insecure in ourselves. Masculine energy penetrates and feminine energy receives. An insecure man who gazes at a woman will never penetrate her. This chapter introduces how to open your woman when you, as a man, still have insecurities. This is challenging and not easy for men to understand.

There are many things happening in the male psyche that need to be overcome in order to achieve the goal of conquering the beloved. I invite you to look at this in reverse. The goal is to get her to open up. The benefit of my being a woman is that I can tell you what it is all about for her. And when you know what it is, you can find better ways to deal with the unknown and become more proficient at opening the feminine. But first I would like you to see and feel it from a female perspective.

Pain closes women

If a woman's natural state is to be open, why does she close up? What pain is she trying to avoid? How many false promises has she had to endure? Why should she think you are any different? Why would she believe you? And be honest ... what will you do when she opens up her flower for you? Will you nurture her seed and thoughts of fantasy? Or will you be blown away by the wind to another flower? If I tell you how to open women, how responsible will you be with this information? These questions I hope you can answer for yourself.

When a man approaches a conscious woman, although she might not be able to articulate her needs clearly, her heart will not lie to her about his intentions. She will feel every inch of your sincerity or lack thereof, and beware, once you open Pandora's Box make sure you can handle the tools you use.

To open, she needs to hear that you are not like her previous lovers. She needs to feel integrity between your words and actions. Her closed demeanour is only a smoke screen for her real deep desire, which is to connect so intimately that she can hardly breathe. A woman's pain will be projected onto you, because until she believes otherwise, you are just like every other male in the male collective to her.

If your behaviour is not what you offered her initially, her radar will detect it and she'll close up. To open she needs to see a little bit of herself in you. She cannot resist her own reflection, if what is reflected is the part that she loves about herself. What she cannot resist will open her.

Arm yourself with confidence

The best weapon with which to open women is confidence. Normally arrogant men approach me and speak to me. Other men, not thinking so highly of themselves, do not approach me directly, because I do not leave myself open. Only men who find the confidence in themselves, deserving or not, have the courage to speak to me. And how can I be impolite once they break through the exterior barrier of resistance? That would reflect my own rude manner to myself. That is sometimes all he needs – an opening created by his own confidence.

Sometimes the poor guy is just ignorant of my subtle walls and is quickly disposed of, but once in a while I have a great conversation with a man, and the next step requires even more skill on his part. Once opened, it is the beginning of a beautiful dance between masculine and feminine that grows to enable two people to connect on more levels than just the physical. It might be his emotional sensitivity that pleases me or his mental stimulation and our overlap of interests. When there is a common spiritual outlook, he is a keeper. And every step in the dance introduces more of him for me to discover.

If he gives up too quickly, I doubt that he could sustain my need to be intimate and intense, and I am saved from another resource-draining experience very quickly. But if he plays with me, we will both grow to discover who we really are together, one step at a time, in a mutually respectful way.

Penetrate her with your focus
A man who cannot gaze at a woman comes across as being insecure. Gazing at a woman is not just looking; it is daydreaming, noticing subtly with deep feelings of desire. Male gazing is the energy-dense, fully focussed observation that a woman feels even before she sees it. It is the type of looking that makes her mushy inside before she can utter her thoughts to herself. And, in the relationship, it is the type of look that makes her want to take her clothes off.

For a man to notice her she has to look radiant; when a man looks, she starts to glow.

A woman opens when she feels beautiful
I heard a story of a woman whose husband died of a terminal illness. This woman's mind was consumed with thoughts of finances and questions of the unknown future that awaited her. The last thought on her mind was her physical need for touch. After a late night chatting and drinking coffee, her male confidant

touched her. Without any resistance or ever considering this kind of relationship even possible, she let him make love to her.

Some might say that he took advantage of her. But to me it demonstrates clearly that a male gaze, even when a woman is unaware of it, addresses her deep desire to be seen as beautiful directly. And just maybe, in a very long time, this was the first time she felt truly open, nurtured, seen, heard and appreciated for being a woman and not for her usefulness. Of course I can say this, because I was that woman.

Do you look at women that way? What are your thoughts during those moments? Do you look only when you know she'll look back? Do you know that there are implications to looking at women in a way that will penetrate them? Doing this will show her your masculinity and bring out her beauty. Or do you think it's too risky to penetrate her now, and you prefer to remain insecure?

Your confidence reflects her beauty

The truth is, gentlemen, the only resistance you will meet in a woman is the resistance she will reflect to you about yourself. If she can look at you and see you as handsome, she has already shifted the part of herself that kept her closed until now. When you feel insecure about approaching her, you need to ask yourself what she reflects that scares you so. How can you deal with those demons? I don't mean in being with her directly. When a man feels too insecure to approach a woman, he still has some stuff to deal with in his own maturing male essence. The irony is that like attracts like, and if the woman you desire keeps rejecting you, you might not be the right match for her. But once you can see and own your own insecurity, you will be able to address her need to feel beautiful. She, in turn, cannot appear beautiful unless she feels it inside.

Healing your insecurity

To deal with your insecurity, you need to resolve your inner resistance when you look at her. To do this you need the greatest love of all: self-love. Then you will transition from being overly concerned with whether she will kiss you back, to it making no difference to you. The proof that you are secure enough to open a woman, is the moment you realise your need to be vulnerable to her accepting or rejecting your gaze. Your vulnerability is the proof that you are confident enough; this is what she will feel and what will allow her to trust you enough to open.

An insecure male cannot open a woman's heart. When you've healed your own insecurities, you'll appreciate her beauty with your gaze just because you can. If she chooses not to acknowledge it, it only comes from her own feminine evolution that is still lacking. The dance of the male gaze and the female's acceptance of it is the ultimate connection. This connection starts a dance between the polarities that spurs a bond of love, until it reaches a stage where it transcends into freedom.

Questions for self-development when you love a woman

- What truth can I tell her about her beauty?
- What resistance do I face gazing at her?
- Where, when and with whom (outside of my relationship) can I share and heal my own insecurity, in order to grow as a man?
- How else can I view female rejection in a way that will assist me to build my confidence?

Chapter 2

❧ When I let go

A love child with no face

Beauty touch my breast

Nurture the seed of soul

Breathe with its movements

Into the depths of my being

Finding peace in togetherness ❧

– Rebirth

Projecting Into The Mirror – The Soul Mate Path

Probably the two most useful concepts to understand in conscious relationships are reflection and projection. Understanding them will help explain why women appear not to cooperate in relationships and why nothing you do can make her happy. At some point we understand that 'happily ever after' is a romantic tale and 'soul mates' is a myth with a hidden purpose. It's a mirror where people project what hurts them onto their partners, which reveals the areas they still need to grow in. Eventually they find out what they were looking for all along – the lost parts of themselves.

Understanding the concept of reflection in relationships explains to men why women leave them and close their hearts. It helps them to grow beyond their frustration with women. To women this inward journey is accepted more easily when they realise they cannot blame their partners for their own feelings, and they allow the inward journey to do what it is meant to do with more acceptance. Both men and women will handle what is happening to them more constructively. Growth develops as the understanding that needs, values, beliefs and boundaries are addressed in ways that expand and respect personal boundaries. Ultimately the feminine emerges with her own voice from a transformation that challenged not only her, but also her relationship with the biggest reflection of herself, you.

Looking into the mirror

When a man can open a woman's heart with his penetrating presence, she feels appreciated for the value she contributes as her gift. Imagine my first husband eyeing me and me responding to his attention positively. I needed to feel appreciated by someone who could open me. In my case, I was fragile and untrusting of men. He offered me the safety of belonging and not exploiting me. And he needed to feel that his attention would be reciprocated. The more he opened me, the more I opened up to the world. I changed my hair colour to blond, wore more expressive clothes and became visible to the world I had tried to escape from. When his friends also noticed me, he protected me from their gazes. We supported each other's needs, which brought us together as a couple. The longer we were together, the more our love grew. Ironically, I believed that a person could only love like this once.

What was happening to both of us was that we were getting to know each other. We were young and open to adjusting to a new mutual lifestyle as we moved in together.

Only in hindsight did I realise that my relationship's purpose was to get to know myself better through my life partner. My partner was a mirror for me to see my own reflection. Imagine looking into a physical mirror. There is probably a wooden support frame that contains glass with a special backing that reflects images on one side.

Two people relating to one another can be compared to a person who looks at a picture in the mirror, and who looks at the actual mirror. The physical mirror is the other person. The image that appears in the mirror, as the reflection, is what the person looking into the mirror sees of him or herself. And the meaning given to the picture reflects the value of the relationship bond. The mirror does not change, but the picture it reflects does.

Consider me looking at my late husband's face, symbolised by the physical mirror and the picture inside: The picture I see in the mirror is his eyes looking back at me, which is my own reflection looking back at me. The quality of this relating is the way his eyes made me feel when he told me that he loved me, or his angry expression when I told him I had crashed his car. What this reflects to me is that I either love myself – when he says he loves me – or that I am angry with myself about the accident I created.

Consider twins who enter and leave a room together. They both engage with the same experience inside the room. But as they come out, one is very happy and the other one extremely sad. Wondering what could create two such different reactions we investigate the room. The room is filled with mirrors. What they saw made one person happy and the other one sad. They both looked at the same things but gave different meanings to them – their very own reflections.

Projection

Recall the physical mirror versus the reflection seen in the mirror to explain projection as well: Do we see the picture reflected to us or a physical mirror? And do we like what we see or do we feel resistance? When I looked at my late husband and I saw a man who was disabled, incredibly intelligent, funny and mentally strong, was I seeing a reflection of myself or was I seeing him for who he really was? If I resisted acknowledging his disability or if it created a resistance within me, this would be a clue to my own projection. Let me explain.

The meaning we give to what we see is our own projection. My late husband was a successful IT student when I met him. He was obsessed with artificial intelligence. He did not allow his disability to hold him back and had newspaper clippings of doing karate despite his artificial limbs. The way I related to him as disabled was possibly a projection, as I saw him through my eyes. I had a history of abuse and abandonment and considered myself emotionally handicapped. We can also call that which influenced my perception of seeing him through my eyes, a filter. From my perspective I admired his success and ability to overcome his obstacles. I looked up to him. What makes my perspective a projection depends on whether I was seeing a physical mirror or a reflection in the mirror. If I had a reaction to what I saw, it was a projection. It was the meaning I gave it that was the projection. For example, did I feel sorry for him or did I admire that he rose above his disability? Would I have a feeling about a physical mirror or a reflection? It is unlikely that I would respond emotionally to a physical mirror. Emotion is normally an indicator that I am projecting my stuff onto my partner. No emotion probably means that I wouldn't even notice a certain perspective.

What makes this even more interesting is that we can have positive and negative projections. What we desire in others is what we recognise about ourselves unconsciously and cannot yet own. Through relating we can learn to pull our projections back as we notice them. Through revealing the shadow and the light, the masculine can see the emerging feminine at last. We experience ourselves in relation to other people – others mirror our existence. The conditions of safety and validation are necessary for us to grow, and unless we develop the ability to pull our projections back, we will not heal ourselves.

Questions to help pull your projections back

- Can I see what triggers that which I reject in my partner?
- Can I recognise this anywhere in my own behaviour?
- How does her behaviour (that triggers me) help her to survive?
- Is it at all possible to understand her behaviour?
- Can I accept this in myself under any circumstances?
- What is the original intention behind the behaviour?
- Is there any way for both partners to serve that need?

Chapter 3

Even if I was not naked

Your stare would penetrate me

Teaching me to receive

Your love

The opposite of intensity

My openness reveals innocence

And purity emerges

An imploding orgasm

– I Cannot Love You if You Do Not Love Me

How Do I Know It Is Love?

Ah love ... everyone can say something about love. And yet it is difficult to define exactly.
There are at least three ways to relate to love:
- Love and compassion for everyone around us
- Love towards a life partner or relationship
- Love for the self

A person cannot have one love without the others – these elements are interrelated. To love a partner, we also love ourselves and feel compassion for those around us. Love is everywhere and in everything and some people say everything is love, including every good and bad experience we go through. Besides the philosophical approach, the question "Do I love her?" still remains. How do you know exactly?

The answer is simply that you can love others only as much as you love yourself.

Does love bring two people together?

Love is noble, but *needs* bring people together. Love is something that develops and grows over time as we relate to each other and fulfil each other's needs. Gary Zukav explains in his book *Spiritual*

Partnerships that the purpose of relationships is to expedite personal growth. I understand that the glue that keeps two people together, before love develops, is what they need from each other. This can be perceived as the feeling that someone loves them. In truth, what we feel for our partners is really a reflection of what we feel for ourselves.

The perception of love is based on need. Love is powerful enough to make the world go round. Relationships tend to trade needs. Love is a feeling that we experience when we learn to accept ourselves more. The purpose reflection serves is for two people in a relationship to reflect consistently what they still need to integrate and accept about themselves.

Love itself is a process of relating to one another. What is felt at the beginning is chemical in nature. The chemistry between people has a physical counterpart in the body. We fall in love with the part of someone that is the same as us. What we discover in the other is a reflection of the self that we appreciate. In approximately 18 months the chemicals that physically bonded you wear off and overlooking misunderstandings and selfish behaviour becomes more difficult. If there is no baby or pregnancy to demonstrate nature's chemical love, forgiveness also disappears as the chemicals' magic wears off. It is almost as if being in love is a booster dose on top of the needs that bring people together, to keep them together if the bond between them is self-sustainable.

When the chemistry is gone, you start to notice all the stuff that is wrong with your partner and the challenges of being together kick in. What you notice are the parts that your partner reflects to you, which you didn't notice when you were in love. When our partner reflects something we are not so fond of, and most probably deny, we think that they are nothing like us. When we realise that this part we don't like can only ever be our own reflection, we experience the growth similar to what Zukav refers to as the relationship's purpose – conscious growth.

The rejected self is the shadow

Any unintegrated part of our self is called a shadow. All the parts of self that we would rather forget about, or reject, because we don't consider them part of who we are, end up in our shadow. The unfavourable aspects we see in our partners are also part of us, but we have rejected them. The person we met and fell in love with is still there, because the physical mirror never changes. At this stage in our relationship, when we reconnect with our lost parts, we will come face to face with our shadow. Our partners reflect our shadow to us to invite us to accept all of them (and all of us) and not judge them. Can we learn to appreciate those parts of our self too as we reintegrate them? This is how love develops as we accept more of our partner and, by default, more of ourselves in the way we relate to one another.

The part of us that was rejected probably occurred at a young age when we were disapproved of as children by our caregivers. When done enough times, we reject these characteristics in ourselves. Unlearning who we think we are, is now required.

Is there enough love to grow together?

Disapproving of our partner is a normal part of the process. The growth spurts in the relationship will continue as we grow together or we break up and grow separately. Some people cannot see the benefit of being together at this stage and go their separate ways, repetitively seeking the in-love chemicals they became addicted to, having unrealistic expectations about love; the love that never got to grow beyond the first stage.

In-love chemicals were designed by nature to bind two people together in order to procreate. The physical bonding and repeated rebonding between partners is created through a flooding of the hormone oxytocin every time a woman experiences orgasm. It is the literal glue that modern society bypasses by using contraceptives. In the event that not enough bonding occurred during this 18-month period, and no babies materialised, the partnership will lack definition and purpose, and may disintegrate. Without the initial chemistry, a continued relationship now becomes a conscious decision.

After the initial bonding period, which is encouraged by the chemical processes, the couple may be pushed into an unconscious decision based on society's expectations. The implication of taking the next step unconsciously is reflected in a 50% divorce rate. If you don't want to be another statistic, you need to start asking yourself some conscious questions about whether you are ready for a commitment like this. If the benefits of the relationship don't outweigh the obstacles, there isn't enough energy to motivate a possible new purpose, even if you both have similar values. This is the time you'll question whether you love this person and define what love is for yourself.

Love reflects how integrated we are
If you love yourself, you'll answer yes to loving the other person. If you don't like yourself much, you'll answer no to loving the other person. How much you love yourself will become clear based on how much you experience this reflection of yourself with your partner. Liking the mirror has little to do with our partners and everything to do with ourselves. Ironically, any person can be the right person. If you don't love yourself and feel compassion for most people around you, you still need to *grow* love. Now, one of two things can happen: you can choose a partner irrespective of the answer to the question, because you can service each other's needs and learn to love yourself and the other person accordingly, or you can leave her and make the choice with a more compatible partner based on what you know you want from a relationship. Very few people can really see their partners without seeing their own reflections. Most people who see their partner's real qualities are able to do so because they are older and wiser and they have accepted more of themselves.

We feel love when we pull our projections back

We find love once we are able to pull back our projection onto our partners. What we think we see in our partner on any good day is but our own reflection. And what we say about him or her is merely a reflection of our internal experience of reality. The day when we can look at our partner, without being triggered by what we would normally not care for, is when we realise that it's possible to accept our partners fully. The truth of it all will allow us to experience their love rather than feel our reaction that we project onto them.

What we blame our partners for is but that which we cannot accept in ourselves. The intensity of the blame shows how much we deny owning it. When we fall in love, the opposite applies, because we still need to integrate what we see in our partners as attributes we also have, but fail to own. As our partners reflect that to us, we welcome how it makes us feel and we really fall in love with ourselves. What we see in our partners are reflections and what we say, think or feel about those reflections is our own projection from our internal reality.

Relationship is a conscious choice

In time our ability to adapt to our environment overrides our choice to continue to do things as we always have, whether we think it works or not. Everyone makes this shift in consciousness at a different time – in their own time and when it works for them. We subconsciously do more of what works and less of what doesn't work for us. By this I mean working towards goals we have or a higher purpose, depending on our level of awareness. Some people will choose their partners despite their individual differences, because they believe they share a common purpose that overrides their differences, to the extent that they will allow themselves to grow into accepting the differences in the other. In a conscious relationship with a purpose to grow, what doesn't work can be viewed as an opportunity to heal what you might consider initially as a difference between you and your partner.

What makes a conscious relationship is a shift in focus. It is natural to form a relationship based on serving one another's needs, but it is a conscious choice to be in a sharing relationship in which you are aware of reflections and projections. Choosing to be with the partner to get to know yourself better is often preferable to not being with your partner. A willingness to grow faster together creates tolerance in a relationship for individuality until there is a readiness to become a natural 'us'.

In Samoan tribes, casual sex is allowed from the time females are sexually ready to explore until they are ready to connect with one partner for the purpose of a creating a family. Women take on the clearly defined gender roles that make the partnership work. By now the young women have already realised their individuality and choose to be with someone to make love and grow a bond of intimacy, to share a life together.

In Western society this kind of tribal behaviour would be misinterpreted and shamed because traditional society expects us to be married before we have sex, so people end up doing things they aren't ready for as they try to find themselves within that relationship.

For men there are no real goals to conquer in a conscious relationship. The opportunities are there for both people to learn more about who they are. And what if the universe conspires to attract you to your complete opposite who owns all the lost parts of you that you haven't yet realised? What better way to have a perfect partner to show you how to love and accept you so that you can love yourself more.

The more opposite to you, the more challenging your partner is to you. This person holds the key to all your lost parts.

Most things are relative; Perspective is everything

To be able to love people we have never met, we would have to be evolved enough to see ourselves in everyone around us. In this context, evolved means that we are learning to see ourselves as love. The relevance is that the more we grow, the more our capacity to stretch our boundaries grows. If I am light, how can I see myself without being in the darkness? If I am standing in the light already, as light, I would see nothing. But when I stand in the darkness as light, I will see myself. That is why reflection is so important to our experience of ourselves as love. We are love. We need to see ourselves as we discover who we are, bit by bit, through our reflections. Then we will grow in love as we accept and integrate more of ourselves.

If we can love anyone we meet with an altruistic, sovereign love how then do we choose a suitable partner with whom we can grow? How do we know it is that kind of love? Not romantic or in love or a god-love, but the kind of love that you develop in a conscious relationship when you get to know yourself intimately.

Choosing a partner who reflects love to us

I often say that from a woman's perspective, we have a binary code of ones or zeros that mean yes or no. This implies that a male starts the process and the female ends it with a no or continues it with a yes answer. So once he has made an offer to her with his gaze, she can accept or reject it. Remember we learnt that this can be a skill that we can improve on to discard the scars from the past, when we realise that she is not exactly a match for us at this time, for reasons of her own evolution. In that way she already makes a choice. The male chooses who he selects to approach with his offer when he is ready. To approach a woman with confidence you need to be sure, and sure of so many things, so you ask, "Is this love? Do I say I love her, and why?" Some of you will say you love her because she said it first. But if you don't feel it, she will know if you are being honest with your feelings. So my tip here is to say it only when you truly mean it.

If you choose the harder but more honest route, you set the first cornerstone for trust in the future. You'll need it when you develop intimacy with each other, which will enable you to be who you really are without any masks.

Choosing the right partner is being with the person who holds your lost parts – your equal and opposite. Some people prefer to trade needs in a working relationship and others choose partners who'll comfort them while they reflect their desirable lost parts to them. And then, of course, it is also possible to play all these roles in the relationship at times, without shying away from being conscious. Trust life to present you with the perfect partner for your soul's evolution.

Saying "I Love You"

If you are the one to suggest you're in love first, you would want to be sure and be the one she selects too. As a woman, when I feel love stirring inside me, I won't show my affection to a man in any way until I feel safe. Maybe it's society or maybe it's the way I learned to play the game, but the female role is one of binary code. And unless the male plays the role of the feminine, which can bring wonderful flexibility to a relationship at times, the female will refrain, for the sake of balance, from being the one to propose love. If women have shared their affections with you before you've done it with them, be aware that you are with women who have a healthy inner masculine and notice the effect it has on you. By masculine I refer to a directive and focussed energy. For some males this is perfectly normal and for others it is not acceptable.

We are all unique and we need different levels of masculine and feminine combinations to balance us so we can live up to our full potential. A very feminine woman will not propose her love until she has been opened by a superior man and is deep into the relationship.

So she chooses you for a partner and you choose her. And the original foundation of love has progressed from a chemical basis, unless there is not enough glue to continue. When there is enough bonding and reasons to keep a relationship together, the real work of love starts.

The work of love

We develop communication skills and make useful meanings to build a steady and solid foundation with a promise to grow, as we learn to love ourselves more through our partner's reflection. Look at the cover of the book and know the one you choose to love reflects the biggest part of you. If you cannot love her, the hardest part for you is that you will spend a life learning to see the love you are in her.

Sometimes we learn to love what we have and sometimes we get the one we loved, before we knew why. It's probably true that if you love her you will do more than you have ever done for her. You may even share a common purpose on higher levels, values and interests. But there is something more. Men generally don't live from their soft side: men are thinkers and plan-makers. Men live from reason and from within their headspace. Women, on the other hand, are intuitive and live from their heartspace. When you learn how to open her with your confidence, more often you will learn to plug into her in a way that allows you to feel completely alive and in touch with the whole universe. Her soft femininity and love allow you to experience yourself as completely focussed and connected to the universe in a way that you could not achieve on your own. When a woman invites you into her soft curves and you connect, your being comes alive and your soul is fed for a while. A woman will put you in touch with your own spirituality as much as you will ground her airy-fairy ideas and help her to act on them. That kind of experience, with the love that it takes to connect in exactly that way, is not just the kind of love you have for your neighbour. I am not quite sure how else to explain this feeling. Can you put it into words? How do you feel it?

Recognise love

For a woman to experience a man's love, she connects with her feelings. It's more than whether you are a good or a strong man; it is not what you are or what you have. Your connection must be deep enough for her to feel herself through your reflection. It is clear that we experience love when we pull our projections back. Until then, all we see is our own reflection. Love is what enables one person to relate to another without it being distorted by judgement or blame and our infatuation with ourselves. It is almost as if there are layers and the foundation is purely two people who are love in their own right. The layer above that is where two people experience their reflections and project their emotions at each other, as if they are each having their own experience exclusive of the other. What keeps them in the same picture is the underlying template made up of the love that they are. But neither of these people can really see one another yet. It is only when they pull their own projections back that they can experience loving themselves.

The male confidence that invited her past the front gate is not love. The sense she gets of you that allows her to feel more than she could feel on her own is an invisible way of feeling through the reflection in a mirror, and projections of the essence of lost love that you contain in who you really are. It is not the gifts of the world you offer her or the words of a serenade, but the feeling of appreciation she gets when you make her feel that she is your special someone. In a strange kind of way this feeling is the feeling she senses of herself, but can never quite see through her current reflections, even though she knows it's there somewhere. It is like looking deep into your own soul and seeing what no one else has shown you, stashed away in the deepest corner of your heart. This is not just any reflection – it is a soul reflection of the lost parts of yourself.

After my divorce I was sure I was completely finished with men. I left for America with a complete focus on spirituality and no goals ahead of me. My life felt like a true love letter to God. I felt and lived like a modern nun and behaved like a Buddha in a bikini. Then I met someone who spoke without words to the deepest part of me, in a way I could not deny or explain logically. I did not act; I only looked up to the sky and asked why I was feeling this way. My mind had to understand an unnamed sensation. I denied what I felt with every fibre in my being. I had a strange sense that he could see right through me. In that moment, all my resistance crumbled even though a relationship made absolutely no sense at that time.

When it is love she feels, she experiences a part of herself as if she is seeing it for the first time. It is not about the person who is right for you, but being ready to experience who you are through another.

And that person then becomes the object of your affection. We experience what we feel through the other's reflections of our self. What is important to remember is that love cannot be denied. When we experience ourselves through another, love cannot be refused.

When it is love she can fight it, but your reaching out will connect eventually in a way that she cannot deny herself. When it is love that you resist, the mind of reason may no longer control you and the time will come when you have to make a choice. At that point the door you open will only be the beginning of a journey you will choose again every day, over and over, as you wake up and decide to court, divorce or be in love with her again.

Questions for him

- Do you find her irresistibly attractive?
- Do you feel new feelings with her around?
- Do you have a different sexual experience every time you make love?
- Are you still in love with her or do you wish you were?
- Can you see a reason to become her life partner besides what you get from the relationship over the long term?
- Does she get to you inside where no one else has touched you before?
- Can you recognise that you have spent enough time with enough lovers to want to be with her specifically?
- Will you do for her what you have done for no other and then some?

Chapter 4

❦ We have now found each other

Across the borders of waters and continents

I wish to express my openness for you

In my human form

Putting the love that I am in a bottle

That when you remove the cork to extract the message

You find a surreal connection with self

Of a sacred intimacy spiraling into the stars ❦

– You Are the Object of My Desire

Is She The One?

One thing people will point out to you when prompted with this question, is that for the right woman they are willing to do something they hadn't done before. When a relationship is conscious, there is a deeper awareness of why she is the one. There is a longing to share time with her rather than be with someone else or alone, despite the fact that you may be in a conflict situation with her. Notice how there might already be a bond. The reason your mind chooses someone specific is because you attract the opposite of your own reflection based on the childhood imprint made by your parents, and you will often notice how your partner resembles qualities of your mother.

A longing to share
More than needing a person because of what he or she has or does for you, there is truly a feeling of wanting to connect with a partner and just be close when you have found your soul mate.

Sharing is a modern notion and probably not one we got from our parents. It is the next generation of meeting each other's needs. I often ask people celebrating their senior wedding anniversaries how they maintain successful relationships. I love asking the men.

The type of answer I get is that "she is always right" or "choosing the relationship over being right or wrong". And when I look at these couples, they appear very harmonious from the outside and often still very much in love with each other.

What I realise is that when we choose one partner for a lifetime companion we really need to understand what sharing means to us personally. What we share and express has many faces and we cannot avoid projecting onto our partners. We can only become aware of our projections.

I question whether relationship needs should be chosen over an individual partner's needs and whether we should choose our need over our partners' needs. If one partner makes a choice, the default assumption is that the choice or need has a higher value than that of the other partner. Asking a conscious partner to make the choice that considers opposite values takes some skill, but the skill can be cultivated. A longing to share within a relationship has many benefits that cannot be experienced outside of a relationship, but the primary purpose of a relationship is not to make us happy.

Take responsibility for your own happiness

Each partner should accept that his or her purpose in life is to learn how to make themselves happy. When making yourself happy puts the other person, or the partnership down, you realise the value of growing towards a clearly defined purpose of what is being shared. This has many lessons that define roles and boundaries that respect the partnership and invite willing and ready partners. If we still expect our partner to make us happy, we are setting ourselves up for a power play.

Know thyself

When we find multiple partners and we have to select one, we need to know ourselves, our needs, desires, personal boundaries, values and beliefs. There are many ways to develop on a personal level, and relationships are certainly one way to escalate that growth. But relationships must not be used with the intention to deal with one's own stuff. We should all respect each other enough to know that certain things are better dealt with outside of a relationship. Some clients tell me that they encounter men or women who want someone to understand them. This is not an unreasonable request but a partner should first try to understand him or herself and develop the skill to express their boundaries, rather than expect a partner to know them. It is subtle, but different. We should all take responsibility to understand ourselves and not expect our partners to do anything we cannot do for ourselves. Don't mistake being in love with personal growth because there is a sense that someone else understands you. This is a typical doctor-patient scenario where a patient 'falls in love'. As you recognise parts you like in the other person, notice how you are seeing a reflection of you and that you are really falling in love with yourself as you hear yourself speak. Act appropriately with your discovery of self and focus the energy where it is required.

Equality avoids games

If someone shares that you are special in some way, accept the compliment and try to see what that person sees. Notice whether the love you display to another, which makes you feel special, is reciprocated. If we admire our partner, this positive projection (which we don't yet own as our lost part) will give our value away to our partner and set up a power play that can later be exploited. Inequality is not a good basis for relationships. Alarm bells should go off for you if she always has to understand that you need time and space to be an individual with individual values. Take time to heal what is yours alone and notice where it is hard for you to respect her values. Most often this reflects how we cannot respect our own values.

Responsibility to deal with your own stuff

In a relationship with a woman, you cannot avoid healing your inner feminine shadow stuff. Test if you can see past your projections. Take responsibility for your part in what is reflected to you. In other words, notice where you experience the emotions when you do what she does. If you can own it, the conflict will dissolve. If you still deny it, get help from a men's group or a professional who specialises in relationships.

A partner who is ready

When we know ourselves, we know exactly what we need from sharing with a special partner. When I met my second husband he knew what he needed. I met him through his work – I had a burglary and he was a loss adjuster. After the insurance claim was settled he asked me out to a movie. I said yes and proceeded to walk to my car to travel to the movies. He walked to his car and raised his eyebrow at me. Being an independent woman in a big city, I didn't see any problem driving there in my own car. Then I realised this was something more formal and I was expected to play the female role. From a distance I asked him what he expected of me. His answer was clear, although funny at the time. He said, "Marriage and four kids."

I was speechless. So before I got in the car I put my request forward, "Please don't touch me." He smiled and we left on the first date of what was to become a relationship.

Express honestly

Don't be afraid to say exactly what you mean – ever. Express yourself with confidence and make sure the manner in which you present yourself will invite what you really want. And know yourself. If you aren't completely sincere she will complain later because she has higher expectations from when you courted her. When what she experiences is different to what she expected, she will be disappointed. Men say things they don't really mean just to impress women. If you love her, you don't want to be in that situation. So be aware of the promises you plant in her psyche, especially if you plan to be with her for a long time. Let everything you say be the truth about you. Rather promise her little and surprise her with much. Don't hide behind excuses because you got distracted and lost sight of your purpose. Women tend to call men on their promises.

A clear reflection
Many men who truly know themselves are also spiritually orientated. They devote their lives to their inner connection with self and often live nomadic lifestyles where they need very few material things. These men tell themselves they know who they are, and they choose not to be with a partner. I have had many conversations with men like these, as I too have been in a place where I felt complete with the masculine and feminine essences inside myself. Then I bumped into my partner almost by accident. So I asked why. "Why, when I made a commitment to myself to be fully self-sustainable, did I meet someone in the physical world to be my partner?" I was rather content with my inner dialogue and the pace of my growth process, like so many spiritually focussed people I knew. The answer was simply that my partner represents *God on earth* to me.

Does your partner represent God on earth to you?

I can imagine your thoughts ... what if a woman looked at me as her god? But it wasn't quite like that. The lesson for me, and here for you, was to truly understand the value of sharing with someone else and I am still learning from these words. For a woman, a man is the reflection of God's masculine side. Could I treat a man with the same respect I would treat God, in the same way that I explained that we could love others, love a partner or love ourselves, to reciprocate with awe? What if the ultimate clear reflection of yourself through your partner is accepting that which you deny the most in yourself? Now the message of God on earth became clearer: I have to learn to look as this very *opposite to me* partner with awe, learning to appreciate those rejected parts of me *that much*.

Mutual respect for values

Can I respect myself that much, and if I do, can I embody it every moment, starting with my partner? What I had to understand was that love doesn't have double standards. Living with an open heart as a spiritual being meant that I was aligned with my feelings, thoughts and actions. And no, this wasn't just in a safe, pure space inside myself. My partner presents me with the ultimate challenge right here on earth every day – to live my true values from the best place inside myself.

Sharing of beingness and understanding lessons

The next level in experiencing the deep reverence and respect of love with my partner, was noticing how he was the one who reflected the best parts of my higher self to me. If and when I could see my partner in that way, I wanted to see myself like that as well. This is part of the true value of sharing and learning through reflection. Sharing with a life partner is not just doing things together or investing in a house together. It is also about how we 'be' together and how we relate to each other, reflecting and pulling projections back. When we meet that special other person, we want to treat them accordingly. We love and appreciate them that much. In observing the deep soul parts of us in the special person we are attracted to so much, we see that those parts are alive and well in us. It is so much easier to love and share in a whole new way when we can accept it.

In other words, if we overcome what we resist in our partners by recognising it in ourselves, our sharing is appreciated in a whole new way.

Integrity of doing

When we do something for our partner, it is because we would do it for ourselves. What we do for our partner is really something we are doing externally so that we can see for ourselves what we need internally. Without doing it, we cannot understand our own inner world. Without understanding why we are doing something for our partner, doing for them creates a feeling of not being appreciated. This is because we miss the conscious awareness of our doing it to get to know ourselves. And if our partner doesn't notice or appreciate it right away – because their focus is elsewhere in that moment – we should not feel rejected. Instead, we appreciate the opportunity that we can share with them in that way. This is a very mature kind of love. In time, relationships can teach us to be fully in our integrity when what we believe is aligned with our actions. The opportunity to have a relationship allows us to pay attention to our partners directly, and indirectly to ourselves, as we learn more about who we are.

Knowing if someone is *the one* is not something you would reason about. You would know if this person is the clearest reflection for you and if the value you give and receive in sharing is what you choose.

Questions that help you to know

- Do you want to do more for her than for anyone else you have ever met?
- Do you prefer to be right or to do what is right for her?
- Do you appreciate her for herself rather than what you want, and see her funny mannerisms as endearing?
- Does it feel like she looks deeply into your soul and really sees you?
- Do you feel like she really understands you?
- Do you know yourself enough to understand what you need and want from her?
- Do you want her enough to tell her you want to be only with her? Do you want to be only with her always? Will she fill your soul?
- Is she the one, but you are not ready?
- Do you respect her more than you do yourself?

Chapter 5

❦ *Be it authentically*

From a place of love

Stay open, alive and raw

Create from this nakedness

A newness that will radiate into the abyss

Of the new reality that awaits

Fear not

It is all perfectly ordained

Supported and thought into being

Here you are now... taking the risk ❦

– Just Feeling It

Am I Ready For This Kind Of Commitment?

Are you ready for the kind of commitment that binds you together when the long-awaited 4-month-old doesn't want to sleep, or your partner's words sound like whining? Those are the questions a man asks before he asks for her hand in marriage. "Am I ready for this?" And he asks it again when he enters his midlife crisis and his libido asks him to notice young and vital-looking females, instead of his partner.

I remember a friend telling me that he was shocked to notice that he found his daughters' friends so attractive. This is quite common for men. Just because the female understands male tendencies doesn't mean she will accept this in her male partner's behaviour. Instead, a couple can deal with their fantasies through sharing. When one chooses to share a private thought, talking about it is a way of acting on it, and sharing a private thought with your partner is preferable to excluding her. If this brings up her shadow stuff, it's an opportunity for healing. She might appreciate you sharing your thoughts more than you know. What does that say about her commitment?

It is said that a man looks for the same thing in every woman and a woman wants everything in one man. Knowing the nature of men and women, what does it take to make a commitment?

What you need to make a commitment

To make a commitment to a beautiful woman, a gentleman requires a guarantee that the merchandise will not lose its sparkle. But his responsibility, once he purchases the merchandise, is to polish it or it might lose its lustre. Remember that what you purchase is affected by how you treat it, and it can improve with age if you invest in it wisely. There is no security in life – merchandise can be stolen if you do not keep it in a safe place.

I realised that everything changes all the time. I was young and it came as a shock to me that the white-collar jobs my parents told me would bring security, did not. I learned instead that everything can change in an instant, and it was up to me to experiment with the truth. Any commitment is subject to the same risks of life, including a lifelong partnership. Happily ever after is not what it appears to be. It requires skills to maintain relationships, founded in the quality of the values that support the commitment we originally made.

Commitment does not entitle us to certain rights. There should still be freedom in how we choose to step into roles. More than anything, it is a commitment to yourself, similar to accepting that your purpose in life is to make yourself happy and fulfil your own needs.

What you commit to

Invest in a partner who understands the rules of sharing, because what you commit to is not giving her a lifelong leash on financial independence or fulfilling her long laundry list of needs (unless of course, this is still part and parcel of what you offer her). A commitment is a journey of personal growth together. The relationship is about getting to know you better and arriving at a place of deep togetherness, acceptance, appreciation, love, compassion and respect. Your partner can only ever be herself and you can only ever be you. No one changes in any way, other than to become more of who they are and true to their nature. That is true freedom. When you connect on emotional, physical and mental levels it is with the kind of intimacy that encourages higher love, just like endorphins after exercise encourage more exercise.

Believe me that sharing also has an opiate effect, which one cannot get enough of with this kind of togetherness; a togetherness that surpasses the chemical bonding of being in love. When your being is flooded with this kind of love and reverence for each other, all the differences and walls are broken down for you to really see each other.

There is an inner knowing

Knowing that you are ready for a commitment that will surpass lifetimes feels like inner peace when you get there. There is a knowing deep inside you that is difficult to explain to other people. You will suspect it from the moment you connect with the right partner for the first time.

When your eyes meet, there is a sense of having been with her even before you met her. Later it is experienced as thinking of each other at the same time, and you are in tune with each other. Have you experienced this?

The responsibilities you commit to

Does being ready for commitment mean that you are not scared of responsibilities? No, it doesn't mean you're not scared. First understand yourself enough to know which responsibilities will be good for you to grow. Some responsibilities might stretch you and, if needed, a conscious relationship will always allow us to be free to choose each responsibility willingly, based on its merits. For example, one of my friends was married for many years before she attempted a family with her husband, despite his needs for a family. He waited patiently until his partner made the decision to have kids. She is a great mom today, despite her independent personality. In fact, the very need she has for independence, with the nurturing environment provided by her husband, has allowed her to fully transcend herself to show up as a nurturer who chooses to do everything with her kids, even when she has excuses to be without them.

What you can expect to get from a commitment

A commitment doesn't bring automatic rights into a relationship because of assumed gender roles. All assumptions can be questioned until the intentions that address the real needs are revealed. Those needs drive the rules and responsibilities. A relationship built on equality deals with resentment and needs in a way that provides space for both partners to grow. Love is the way we relate to each other. If we love each other, we will be gentle with one another's hearts. We notice our behaviour and adjust it according to the highest purpose in that moment, as we stay in the present moment, forgiving and forgetting past pain.

Being ready for a commitment doesn't come without clearly defined boundaries. To declare boundaries we need to know ourselves and, in the process of getting to know ourselves, we need flexibility to adjust them according to both parties' needs.

Breaking commitments

There is one more comment worth making about commitments. After I got divorced and left for the US on an extended visit, I met a wise Indian who asked me how I could break my marriage vow to my ex-husband. I guess in a way he was confused about my spiritual outlook, which was, from his perspective, a selfish need to be free. Knowing what I know now I cannot presume to speak of commitments in ignorance of the truth, and I'll address here what I realised.

At the time, when the knowledge came that I had to be on my own, it was accompanied by the same kind of feeling I had when I met my ex-husband. As if I woke up from a long dream, I just knew my life with my current partner was over; it was as if a sacred contract had ended. I had two boys who needed nurturing from both parents, so I asked myself many questions. The first question was whether I'd made a mistake or misunderstood my guidance at the time I committed to my partner. The answer was a clear no because I did exactly what I needed to do. I can look at it now and also say that there are no mistakes, only decisions. I also know, in the same way I know I have ten fingers, each time I look at my beautiful boys, they needed to be here in this world. At the time, I accepted that the answer would not be revealed until I was ready to understand it, and I had to learn to trust what I felt. The only thing that made sense to my logical mind was that there was a higher purpose on my life path. I had to be freer than I was at the time, even though I had no way of understanding it then. Writing this, years later, I can honestly say I am as in the dark now as I was then when it comes to logical reasons. What I do know and accept is the growth that would come for both of us.

I find that since I have grown, I connect more deeply with my new partner emotionally and spiritually, as well as physically and mentally. In no way would I have engaged in such a relationship had I not experienced this deep healing. I had to heal, and for as long as I blamed my partner for what I couldn't do for myself, which was to accept myself completely, healing could not happen. There was no safe platform for me to be vulnerable without defending myself, and I didn't know how to learn what I did, living a life that asked me to be what was not enough for me to be me anymore. Yes, I was selfish. I acted like a child. Now I have to explain it to my children every time I see them. I was not ready for the commitment or the responsibilities of parenthood when I made the decision. I did what women do when they feel pain and reject themselves: I withdrew and then disappeared from my world, as I knew it. I could no longer recognise all that I created as mine.

What part of me created all that? Did I ever do it for me, the me who was now being revealed? Maybe I was going through my very first initiation (which I refer to in Part Three of the book). I had to break away from my parents' projected dreams and fears that had been transferred to my ex-husband. I was no longer willing to please other people if it did not also feed my soul. I wanted to claim my own dream even when I had no idea what I could do after ten years of nurturing children. I realised I didn't know how to nurture myself. I didn't even know myself. Who was I now? And I couldn't blame my ex-husband for any of it. I broke a marriage vow because I understood that my soul's desire at the time was to be free of the expectations of other people. If I had been ready for a commitment in the first place and hadn't tried to put a plaster on the pain of being abandoned by my first husband's death, I may have been willing to take on the responsibilities of a conscious partnership and the role of mother. The quality of my connectedness with my ex-husband was a substitute for what it could be and I did the best I could.

But this only worked until I realised that the real purpose of the relationship (to know myself) could not be fulfilled by the rules set up in my relationship. So much of me still had to heal and be discovered to know who I was. Anais Nin said that when the pain to remain tight in a bud becomes more than the pain required for growth, the flower will open. For me it was like waiting until my circumstances allowed me no other choice than to move instantly through whatever had to heal inside me, to learn how to transform knowledge into wisdom. Although I was searching all over the world, I could not see what was in front of me, because I was not ready to see myself. If I hadn't left the relationship, I might still have been under the impression that it was my ex-husband who failed me and I would never have taken responsibility for myself. Being alone, I finally got it and I healed.

It takes two people to make a commitment
To commit requires clarity of mind about needs and expectations, and the boundaries and rules you make together. I broke off my marriage because as I came to know myself better, I wanted to be free to be me and live from inside my heart rather than step in the role that was prescribed for me. Don't expect your partner to follow you, rather have her follow you because you earned her respect.

It is so important to allow for growth in a relationship after you make a commitment. The person you're committing to will change as they discover or deny who they are. Today my ex-husband and I have a wonderful friendship and are great parents to our children. I could never repay him for the gift of growth. I sacrificed much materially to gain self-respect to commit to being the best me I could be. For me to experience the growth process of living according to my heart rather than doing what was expected of me (outside of me), I needed to change my circumstances. I waited for a long time for him to say or do the right thing accidently that would reflect what I needed, because I didn't know what I needed. In reality, I couldn't expect him to do what I couldn't do for myself. No matter how hard I tried, it just didn't work being in the same environment. My heart was already too closed from past pain I had felt and from seeing him as my enemy.

A woman who is ready to commit will know herself and what she needs. A woman who doesn't know what she needs is still attached to the projections of what others think she should be. She will never be truly satisfied and nothing you do will satisfy her for long. A commitment that lasts a lifetime requires both people to know who they are and to stay connected as the relationship develops. If this is acceptable, and even desirable, maybe we are mature enough to deal gently with the resistance inside ourselves.

Only love has the power to break down walls. The walls only break down when we are ready to receive our soul lessons. As we integrate the lessons and we choose to let go of boundaries that are no longer required in the relationship, the walls disappear. Sometimes the walls still need to be there to get to know ourselves within the walls, before we can let them go.

It takes two people to commit to a relationship with the required boundaries in place to get to know who they are. Accepting the boundaries and responsibilities is what makes a commitment. If only one partner commits to responsibilities, this becomes a conscious codependence.

Questions to find out if you're ready

- How prepared are you to grow together?
- How much will you be willing to co-create outside of your individual needs?
- If it is still just about you, don't need more time to grow as an individual before you commit?
- What do you want from this commitment?
- Do you want a family?
- Do you need assets like housing together? Would you want to commit if those things were not necessary?
- What about finances? Will you still be willing to make your own way or are you depending on your partner's share?
- Do you know what it means to commit for a lifetime, or do you just want to commit until the mutual respect disappears?
- Do you understand that any resistance you have towards a possible commitment is inside yourself?
- Do you know yourself well enough to explain the kind of relationship you desire?
- Do you know what exactly you are committing to? Does it have conditions or is it life-long?
- What responsibilities are you willing to take on?
- What relationship responsibilities will you not take on?
- Are you prepared to be responsible for your own happiness in the relationship?

- Are you willing to accept your partner as a reflection of yourself?
- What will you lose by not committing to this relationship? Were you previously aware that you had this hidden need?
- Can you accept your partner exactly as she is?

Chapter 6

His hand is

Warmly placed on my inner thigh

Soft and inviting, my body and I are one

Firmly forces open what he wishes to claim

I feel the earth's pulse

As he pushes his body against mine

My back is arching

My heart is opening again

– Rejection

What Is Codependence And How Do I Avoid It?

Looking through the conscious relationship lens, we discovered how the simple act of looking at a woman has value. Once the woman has been opened, you find yourself looking at a reflection, a reflection you question whether you love as you struggle with the interplay of self-acceptance and denial. In relationships, this dance of opening and closing each other's hearts brings us closer to feeling intimately close or rejected. Sometimes, when we've opened and made a commitment, we may not want to let go ever again.

It is time to explain the risks of codependence. Old-school roles create the foundation for codependent relationships, where males assume the role of financial provider and women nurture children as part of their socially acceptable and defined participation.

Codependence starts out rather innocently, as we give our power away over time to our partner. The more dependent we become, as we expect them to fill their roles, the more we need them to do what we gave up doing for ourselves. Gradually we lose our confidence and the drive to do things for ourselves and we cannot live without them.

Taking responsibility provides a platform for equality

For a conscious relationship to be equal, each partner has to be willing to take full responsibility for themselves. This is very different to the long laundry lists women have, or males seeing females as token trophies. When love overrides all inequality in a relationship and two people want to share equally, there is no codependence, even when one partner contributes more than the other.

Acknowledging value keeps equality in place

When a man resents a woman because she is at home with the kids while he provides, certain things start to happen that create codependence. The codependence creates a power play.

Love cancels out the control games people use to get what they want in relationships. Only in love can real needs be met. At some point, the one who has more gives from a place of love and the one with less adapts to this lifestyle. This is how the dependence can be created unconsciously. If the one who gives expects constant appreciation, or the one who has less sees it as their right to have some of what the other partner gives, inequality can create co-dependence.

Express needs and be prepared to fulfil them yourself

To address inequality we have to be willing to express our needs honestly in that moment. As she expresses her needs honestly, she realises how she can meet her own needs most of the time. At one time, my partner reminded me that I could go back to the corporate arena to contribute to our lifestyle. From my point of view, I felt that I was contributing so much emotionally to my family and my office that I could not sustain myself if I also worked full-time. I preferred to adjust my lifestyle to a more conducive working environment that catered for my needs and values but failed to express it to my partner.

I now had two small children since I last worked under pressure in full-time employment. I had no way of understanding at the time that I needed to show that, in return for my financial security, I provided the emotional buffer that made the family unit work. I feared that if I did express it, its value would not be accepted in society as it had no apparent monetary equivalent. Would the exchange have been considered fair? My relationship needed to appreciate the finer skills I had now developed. Instead of a new agreement, my marriage changed into a codependence that I had to break in order to value myself and accept who I was. I lacked the maturity to address my need to be appreciated for my emotional input, and feared the resentment of my partner. This demonstrates clearly the need for new agreements when the roles change, to avoid codependence. In this case, my lack of expressing my need kept me from realising how I could fulfil it myself.

There are times when good communication cannot fix a relationship but calibrating values can
Everyone has a specific set of values, which is at the core of their personalities. People would rather change their partners than what they believe. Ken Wilber and Martin Ucik jokingly said in an interview that no matter how good the communication in a relationship, when people are grouped according to their values and fall into different value groups, they need more than communication to deal with certain issues.

A couple benefits from a similar order of thinking, or an unspoken agreement, that makes up their values. If a relationship is conventional and works because two people agree to fulfil certain needs for each other, it is a codependence that works. But if two people enter into a conscious relationship in which each person takes responsibility for their own happiness, and decide to share a common purpose, the next generation of relationships has arrived. A higher order of thinking is present to which two people hold themselves accountable, and this goes beyond communication skills.

Codependent relationships are not natural bonding
Connecting has many aspects, just like there are physical, emotional, intellectual and spiritual aspects to a person. Bonding with a physical connection could very well be codependence by choice, but does not have to be transactional.

An emotional connection takes the relationship to the next level. It requires an open heart. In the past, intuition was considered a feminine trait since sensitivity was more common in females than males. Accordingly, nurturing was given by women; their bodies' softness even reflects this attribute. Today, more and more men connect at this level, as they get in touch with their inner feminine. In fact, women prefer men who are emotionally sensitive. This doesn't mean you have to cry in front of her, but that you have the listening skills she requires to be heard and seen without you having to fix her.

There is also the potential for a mental connection. I'm not only talking about sharing intellectual interests, but the ability to connect with one's partner in their physical absence. Often in my life I've had mental connections with partners or clients. Codependence is neediness in an unequal way. Bonding is a way of connecting and it holds more potential for the relationship.

Many healthy ways to connect
A woman opens to the male for the purpose of experiencing life intimately. In many ways she also performs a dance of seduction with the world. What makes her feminine is the way she chooses to engage intently and listen with presence to the heart song of another, so something inside her connects with them. I experience a knowing at times when someone thinks of me. I can text them and confirm this knowing with a returned text smile or a message that said that they just spoke of me. Call it a sixth sense or

intuition, but to me it's a mental connection one makes with another. When I experienced chatting to sensitive people on Facebook, I often felt drained. Later I observed how I used my energy around these people. Sometimes I chose to cut off people who connected with me because of how they *felt*. We are all responsible for our energy and if people leave us feeling drained we have a responsibility to ourselves not to create codependencies. Keep this kind of connection for your partner where it belongs; in a healthy environment in which it is respected.

There is another type of spiritual connection that some people will feel in their lifetime. There is a deep knowing of each other that may feel familiar. It is an awareness of sharing lifetimes together and a memory of events and feelings. Once, when feeling stuck in my marriage, I consulted a regression therapist. In this experience I learned that my partner and I were related in a previous lifetime. Without the need to share personal details I can convey that the bonds we make often span lifetimes. Sometimes we have contracts that need to be fulfilled and there are parts of ourselves that need reintegration.

There are various kinds of spiritual contracts. Not all are with partners and not all connections we feel with people are because we were lovers in other lifetimes. We are slow learners and might need many lives to learn one soul lesson. I believe that for us to be the best that we can be, through a process of acceptance of people and what they reflect to us, we will eventually integrate all the parts of our souls here on this planet. And reintegrating those lost parts is our responsibility. When we leave here, we take nothing with us except how much we evolved on our soul journey.

I wonder why there are so many broken marriages and multiple partners today. In the past, our parents spent a lifetime with one partner to learn from. What if we were to heal much more of ourselves in this lifetime, more than in others? It seems logical, but then it also seems logical to choose a partner who connects with us on as many levels as possible – mentally, emotionally, physically and spiritually.

Now just imagine what it is like to connect physically with a partner when you know your spiritual purpose together, are emotionally present for each other, and connect mentally.

Questions

- What do you expect your partner to do for you?
- Can you be you without the service your partner provides for you?
- Would you like to be independent or not? What is your preference?
- Is there room in your relationship to go to the next level of a conscious relationship?
- Do you connect mentally with each other?
- Would you like to be emotionally present for your partner?
- Do you feel your partner's neediness? What does this reflect to you about yourself?
- Can you pull your projection back and renegotiate an equal agreement for your relationship that respects both partners' values?
- Are you free to give yourself what you need?
- Is your partner free to say no to what you ask them?

PART TWO

Understanding How

Conscious Relationships Work

Chapter 7

The bottom of the hole

Truth a fairy tale

Face to face with darkness

Seeing only the smile

From within the lie exposed

Nothing matters

Love prevails; Paradox frees

For I am no one

And no one knows me

I could be anyone

Anyone but me

– Indifferent

Whose Stuff Is This Anyway?

The first part of this book addressed masculine and feminine needs to create the values for living a conscious relationship. Part Two discusses the process of relating with conscious awareness between two people. What will you face during the cycles of growth?

The very first, and often the most confusing element, is understanding who is to blame for what went wrong. Or put consciously, who needs to deal with their stuff, to relate to each other, within the conscious values we described earlier? Remember you won't be reading books or asking questions if everything in your relationship is working. Similarly, we all know not to fix what is not broken. Read this chapter with an open mind and the outcome might surprise you.

Understanding rules in conscious relationships

We live in a society in which we're not used to making rules. Rules *just exist* and we obey them. If we want to be in a rock band we first learn to play classical music, as we need to learn structure before we can be creative with it. We don't quite understand what it means to co-create in a relationship because we never learnt to create a relationship from scratch – we were just given the rules.

Our model for relationships comes from our parents. Since we're taught by conditioning, we don't question the rules. As young kids we learn to pass on blame: to kick the wall when we walk into it and not take responsibility for our part in it. When we don't understand the rules that make a system work, we look for someone to tell us what they are. We follow the rules until we realise that we can participate actively in making rules as we discover and understand the intention behind the rules.

This conditions us to believe that we have to be right or are in control, which implies by default that our partner must be wrong. If we obey the rules, we are free of accountability. Our generation has a disease of always looking for a scapegoat – which short-circuits our potential to grow. The moment we can pass the buck, our thoughts let go of the perceived problem we need to solve. This is the crucial point that makes the difference between whether we can progress to the next level or not. If we cannot see a good enough reason to question the rules, we always follow them instead of making them. Making rules means that we have to understand the original intention they were created for in the social system. That is co-creating responsibly.

Encountering new perspectives brings new rules as you look at the way your own relationship works.

To know if it is your stuff you need to know yourself

The first qualifier to be in a conscious relationship is to be an individual with your own identity and knowledge of self, separate from other people's views of you. This implies that you have a known unique personal structure. Hopefully, you're able to sustain yourself, implying that you understand the *rules* of how you *work* and have the ability to express what you need. You enter into a relationship as this known individual structure and become one with another unique personal structured individual. As such, two separate individuals now have shared needs and resources and will divide roles and tasks to co-create in their environment. What makes it conscious is being aware of how male and female assumed roles might serve you. In a co-creation we make our own rules and, as we change, our needs change.

If you don't know who you are, learned rules can divide you
Did you know that rules exist to allow us to play a game safely just like they do in sport? Did you know that St Augustine made Christianity a religion about 300 years after Jesus lived in order to keep the peace between opposing spiritual views at the time? In the same way, years later General Smuts in South Africa was slain because he created legislation to avoid violence between Europeans and non-Europeans. What these two historical events have in common is that they used rules to create separation to serve a certain purpose. Rules divide us when they are no longer apply to the original purpose for which they were intended. Our old-fashioned way of thinking about the roles in relationships no longer seems to apply when it creates a power struggle and inequality in relationships. Breaking codependence is sometimes essential, until partners can co-create new rules that are as individual as their needs in the relationship.

Needs can be clearly identified and stated between partners. Acknowledge each other's needs and put new agreements in place, that serve the current needs, to address mutual responsibilities. Until there is accountability, the relationship will experience bouts of blame as one person passes the buck to the other from an assumed right, according to old rules that are no longer valid.

To avoid blame, one needs to be big enough to know that it takes two to tango, and if there is any hint of blame, both parties need to identify their part and take responsibility for it.

Projecting is your stuff

Projecting, as described before, happens when we project our opinions of what are really our own reflections of self onto our partners. We communicate it in sentences that start with, "You are ..."

A father who has dyslexia will relive painful experiences when his 10-year-old son arrives home with poor reading test results. If the father reacts in a way that seems unreasonable or inappropriate, like being angrier than is required about the poor mark, he is said to be projecting. If the teacher contacts the parent and asks that something be done, the father might feel pain for his child, not realising it's his own unhealed experience he's reliving. The father might even suggest that the child be prescribed medication, rather than address the actual problem. In reality, the only action required by the teacher is some extra attention for the child's study time. In this example, the father projects his own experiences of shame onto his child and feels sorry for him. His reaction to medicate shows his own projected feelings trying to protect his child. If he is able to pull his projection back, he'll hear the teacher saying the child needs extra study time.

In relationships, projections are often linked to intense defensive feelings and we cannot hear our partner's real need. The communication might start innocently, telling a story, but our partner hears past pain, through her own filters and experiences, rather than hearing the actual facts. The clues we're looking for are the hidden feelings that are coming up. Attributing our values to our partners by saying, "You are ...", is not as accurate as asking them if we can assume what we are thinking. For example, saying, "Can I assume that you ...?" is a more constructive comment to make when trying to open your partner. Attempts to defend our statements are clear indications that we are protecting our feelings. Feelings indicate stuff – your stuff.

Blaming is a signal that it is your stuff

One partner will blame another for doing something that caused her pain. Sometimes the one receiving the blame is unaware of the pain. As the partner states her opinion, the person being blamed could perceive it as an attack. Confusion sets in as a lot of information is required to correct the internal maps that create not only this behaviour, but the pain that is felt. Of course, if the person projecting has it pointed out to them, it will infuriate them even more. Any defensive response or lack of acknowledgement of their feelings will leave them unable to even perceive that the blame is already a projection on their part. In this sense, it is seldom wise to pursue any attempt to address the issue in the moment and preferable for the one who is projecting to notice their own emotional, irrational behaviour. To find out what the unhealed event was in order to work with it consciously, the best response is often none at all. This happens often in relationships and there is always the opportunity to grow and get to know oneself. The best approach is to stay open to listening and receive a partner's comment with love and tolerance, and to enable the person to see their own mistakes. Most of the time what we blame our partners for is exactly what we are doing.

Any need to defend yourself means you're not dealing with your stuff

Any defensive behaviour will be like fuel on a fire. In his book *Intimacy*, Osho said that the shadow side of awareness is self-judgement. I didn't understand this until I experienced it myself. When I completed my final boot camp assessment for my meta-coaching qualification, I realised that I express everything I say for my own ears to hear, for my own benefit. The biggest lesson was that every word I thought about other people was some kind of projection of my own stuff. As a result, I was silent for two days with little to say after coaching. I heard myself saying things about me, things that in the past I would think I was saying about other people, for their benefit, but now realised were reflections of me I could not own. I defended my opinions because I couldn't accept what was said about me. When we hear someone speak about us and we have an understanding that there is no need to take it personally, because this person is really speaking of themselves, there is no need to respond. The need to defend ourselves indicates that we haven't accepted what we are accused of and that part of us is still rejected inside, meaning that we have stuff to deal with.

Every part reflected at you that you deny is your stuff
First we notice that everyone is a reflection for us to learn who we are in this world. With each reflection you choose to accept that part of yourself or not. As we choose to reject certain parts of ourselves, as if it isn't who we think we are, we encounter the first step in personal mastery: Taking this step it would be spiritually arrogant to assume that we can be vulnerable by being wrong as a judgement of self or others. During these times humility is necessary and appropriate if we wish to learn that what we think is wrong also served us at some point.

The first time I read that Jesus got angry in the temple and made his own whip to remove people selling in the temple, I was shocked. Could he really do that? For me, it was unthinkable that it could be acceptable to be angry, let alone it being Jesus.

What we think we are not or what we reject in ourselves, we will continue to project onto others. When we come to understand that every attribute serves us in certain situations, we discover that we are *all things and all qualities*, and it is up to us to use them wisely and appropriately to serve us. It can be seen as morally wrong to steal, but not if it's for a child who will die if he doesn't eat. If we can express our need honestly and just ask for what we need, it is possible the owner of the potentially stolen goods will part with them willingly.

Every action has a positive intention if we can find it
Every part of our personality aims to serve our needs as a human, and it is up to us to act from the highest part of ourselves. The better we know ourselves, the easier it is for us to say no without it creating unnecessary pain in another. We don't hurt people intentionally, rather they hurt because of unhealed pain from the past reflecting back to them. As we evolve in our process of growth and take our power back, we discover the truth. No matter how hard we try, we can neither hurt nor satisfy another. Their emotion comes from their experiences and beliefs.

Emotions are the alarm bells warning us that we have stuff to deal with
So when we ask whose stuff it is, we aren't looking for someone to blame. Nor are we looking to avoid our responsibility for the part we had in creating the experience. We cannot take our partner's pain away from what they project. The only logical approach is to be present and witness our partner's journey of personal growth, as they realise their own projections. Every emotion we have about another is but a reflection of ourselves. I know this is difficult to understand at first. I now also know that even though I asked my ex-husband for the need that mattered most to me (that he accept me for who I was), I was the person who was truly not ready to do it. I couldn't accept myself as I was. So I went off to Peru and then Hawaii to find myself in vision quests. Even when we ask ourselves whose stuff it is, the chances are good that is our own. We need only look inside to find the answer we seek.

Relationships are mirrors we look into to see our stuff
I used to think that relationships were just there to serve as excuses to blame our partners for that which we could not fix in ourselves. In part, that was true; relationships make it so much easier to see in another what I fail to see inside myself. James Swartz, who wrote

How to Attain Enlightenment, says that relationships are problems. He is not wrong, but relationships are also opportunities to share, outside of ourselves, experiences of deep connection and love in its many facets as well as some experiences that being single does not offer us at all. Life always presents us with choices and the free will to live it the way our souls desire.

The stuff belongs to the one with the emotions.

Unless your partner is an empath (someone who feels someone else's feelings) she cannot always know what you feel. The responsibility is yours if you decide to go on the relationship journey. There is no end destination; the only solace I can offer you is that with more awareness comes more self-judgement, until you learn to love yourself more and can pat yourself on the back for being honest and not getting stuck in negative emotions.

When it's not your stuff you still have a role to play
If your partner is aware that it is her stuff, the role you play first is that of witnessing. It helps if we can be present with our partners with love when they experience their pain. Any feedback only needs gentle prompts for awareness. Being in a conscious relationship makes her vulnerable and will put her in a space of self-judgement, so she requires compassion from her partner. It is a very useful skill to bring safe boundaries into the relationship, to protect virtues like not judging each other for mistakes made and forgiving each other before the mistake is made. When I read *The Shack* I was overwhelmed by laughter and acceptance when people related to each other. It demonstrated that even if it was a story of how God is depicted as a black woman, there are no limits to the value of acceptance for one another just as we are. And even if

we're still looking for the fault in ourselves, or others, we can at least verbalise and strive for a higher way of being. Einstein said if we can imagine it, it exists somewhere, and I believe that too. Imagine what relationships would be like when we focussed our awareness on what is working instead of what is not!

Forgiveness
On a higher level, there is a love strong enough to forgive every time, to not hold anything against our partners as they grow, and maybe that is the potential of a conscious relationship if we can keep on the journey.

Once I asked the angels if there was a soul mate out there for me. They replied that I could only see him if I could live without judgement. Judgement means that one person is right and the other person is wrong. As long as we think we are right, it implies another is wrong.

On this journey I came across Rumi, a thirteenth century poet who said, "Beyond our ideas of right-doing and wrong-doing, there is a field. I'll meet you there." To live in a conscious relationship we need to know ourselves; and love ourselves just as we are, without judging who is wrong or right. We make our own rules and we take responsibility for ourselves, and our own happiness. What is left to share is a pure connection innocent of one another's stuff. Looking inside and finding those hidden parts of self becomes a process to grow our love of self and our humanness.

When you do look inside you will pass the point where you start wondering whose stuff it is and who is right or wrong. Asking the question, "Whose stuff is it?" can prompt us to look at ourselves first. Remember to be gentle with compassion in your heart when you find the answer. Maybe in time we can reach a point of being so integrated that there is no reason to forgive our reflection or ourselves because we really did nothing wrong. We can comprehend that the decision we made was the best we could at the time, and that is completely acceptable with nothing to forgive the self or others for.

Questions

- Do you recognise your participation in your experiences of what appears as a struggle in your relationship?
- Do you still blame your partner for your stuff?
- Do you notice when you are defensive and try to protect your hidden fears and pain?
- How do you identify your own projections?
- Can you recognise and be accountable for your own role in what triggers your partner's emotions?
- Do you judge yourself harshly?
- Can you see how judgement might not serve your relationship?
- Can you have compassion for your partner's growth?
- Do you credit your own awareness and capacity to hold space for your partner to grow?
- Is your focus to look for the faults or what is working when relating to your partner?
- Can you notice if the rules you live by still serve their original purpose? Are you empowered to change them? Which ones can you change as your needs change?
- Do you notice any blind spots at all?
- Can you allow these areas of growth to become the potential to love yourself (and your partner) more?

Chapter 8

How do you ask this of me?

I am in pain

Can you not see my wounds?

Breaking the patterns of my habit

From victim to victor

Transformation of choice

Claim it she says

It is up for grabs

But did I deserve it

– Putting Soul back into Life

Will I Ever Break Through This?

At times in the relationship, as you become more attuned to and aware of the issues, you will wonder if you can break through the issues that seem so very persistent. The feeling that accompanies this knowing is one of entrapment, a sense that you are not able to move forward. You are committed to your partner and you know she might never change. You know the answer is to come to a place inside yourself where you accept it all. Instead, you would rather give up and walk away, because it seems as if it'll never move beyond this point where you feel stuck.

Drawing wisdom from knowledge
It is time to return to a place of innocence in the relationship. If, for all your awareness, you feel that you have exhausted your resources, there is wisdom in knowing when you need time out, or knowing when you need nurturing, just for you. During these times it is better to go inside, rather than try to force some kind of breakthrough in the relationship, or to walk away and do some self-reflection of your own.

We already know that keeping an open mind and a loving heart are more useful than resisting what we face, despite our current capacity for patience. Good intentions and an honest approach in communicating still don't prevent the same situation presenting itself again. Still we have to resist the internal feelings of fixing the problem rather than accepting it. Our knowledge here works against us, and knowing is not enough. It is exactly this learned behaviour of doing something that creates the mental struggle at this point. If we aren't able to do something, we feel helpless. But there is another way: allow the problem to become the solution, by doing nothing.

Choose your focus: Energy flows where attention goes
Have you ever focussed so much on a problem that the solution stays just out of your range of vision? So far, our reasoning based on knowledge has brought us to a subtle yet negative slant in the discussion. At this point, it is already obvious that to break through anything we first have to realise that our perspective about a glass of water should be neither half empty nor half full.

Often the meaning we make of something holds more power over us than the facts themselves.

To decide if the glass is half full or empty when it is still just a glass of water, can be directing our energy in a way that prevents us from seeing the solution right in front of us. When we focus so much on the problem (what we now decided was a half-empty glass), the mind perceives just a glass of water as an obstacle. It is the very same glass of water that can be both half-empty and half-full, and the interpretation (half-empty) means that we separate the facts from the meaning. The meaning itself locks us into an interpretation that, when we can't overcome it, gets bigger the more we focus on it. The bigger it gets, the less we see past what is between us and the solution we seek. We are now focussed solely on the obstacle.

Where we put our focus is the second clue to breaking through anything. Whether we focus on the end of the line, or see the obstacle on the way there first, determines to a large extent what we will notice around us during that time.

If we are focussed on the meaning, we will notice, in our environment, more of the same type of meanings (negative or positive) that get in our way.

When we focus on the solution at the end of the line, we notice viable solutions in our environment that are available immediately.

On a practical note, start to notice the words you use in conversations. Words are the clues we leave to indicate if we see the glass half full or half empty. We use self-prophesising words. If we can become aware of the words we use to describe what we feel stuck about, they will indicate where our focus limits our ability to see the solution, and we can choose to focus on something else. We direct our energy with words as much as actions, which makes it easier or harder for ourselves. When our words are positive, they reflect our underlying beliefs. Our beliefs shape our perceptions and experiences of reality, whether we are aware of them or not, and we express our beliefs through our use of language and words.

Attitude determines a positive outlook

In *Unlocking the Mystery of Happiness*, a book by Diener & Diener, research revealed that most people experience the same type of events in their lives. For some people, because of the way they choose to view their life, theirs is a happy life and for others it's a depressing one. The attributed value of happy or depressed is what we decide about our experiences; our perceptions and beliefs determine our experience of life.

How we think about our lives is reflected in the words we use to describe them. So referring to our relationships as obstacles or opportunities already shows us a lot about our outlook and we can focus and make meaning based on where we place our awareness.

Get all the facts and observe them without making any meanings, if possible, to get to the right attitude for a breakthrough.

Values and beliefs create perspective

The relevance of known facts, before we make meanings about them, still depends on our general outlook and our level of awareness at the time. As a coach, I've gained a reputation for being able to break through stuckness with clients. As much as I understood the value of a changed and more positive perspective (by seeing the glass as half full rather than half empty), I realised that there was as much value in just noticing the glass of water as *a glass of water* without making any kind of interpretation.

Often this awareness introduces something new and healing into the conscious conversation where you and your partner both connect in a way you desire. Somehow, when met by the truth before the personality takes on a viewpoint, you encounter the sacred moment when two people stand back from their chosen values and self-limiting beliefs.

We remember how people make us feel and not so much the facts or stories that surround the emotion. It was these repeated moments that allowed me to see how a feeling of being stuck was just a perspective. The facts are the facts, and as long as we can see them without taking a stand about them, there is no stuckness. Keep this in mind when you choose to answer the question "Will I ever break through the perceived obstacle in the relationship?"

Your partner's role when experiencing stuckness

As a partner your conscious role is not fixing it for your partner as you have been conditioned to believe, but to be the preferred witness of your partner's experience of growth. Feeling stuck can be painful or, if not perceived that way by the other partner, may not have any attached feelings or awareness at all. Each person shifts through problems at their own pace, in their own time, and according to their own level of awareness. So if you are the one with the awareness of being stuck and you are the one experiencing the pain, I would like to suggest that you look within yourself for the hidden underlying lesson of letting go of your point of view and noticing the facts. The person experiencing the frustration is the one who has stuff around it. If one can let go of *expecting* the partner to break through this, the attached pain will go away. It makes it easier if we realise and accept that all things happen in divine right time.

Introducing the value of a spiritual understanding

Religion is not spirituality. Religion is a belief system of our choice that links us to a power higher than our conscious minds' perceptions. Spirituality refers to a set of values we hold as our truth because they are held in place by experiences that confirm what we believe. This may or may not include the belief in something bigger than ourselves.

The difference is that religion is represented by a set of given rules on right and wrong and spirituality is based on our own understanding, which is prescribed by us alone, and may or may not be underpinned by a belief system (or a few). For the purposes of this book, I need to clarify my own position, as I often refer to something bigger than me in terms of various religious belief systems from Christianity to Buddhism. I also refer to God as the Divine, the Universe, God Source, guides, angels or a higher self. The word God has existed for only a thousand years. I pray that my choice of examples will not offend any belief system of your choosing, but rather allow you to find the value of the message to relate to your own frame of reference. I chose to quote authoritative sources, poetry and philosophy because sometimes I agree with their views, but at other times I find it necessary to challenge them.

Every breakthrough requires that we learn a spiritual lesson
One way to solve the problem is to recognise the spiritual lesson behind the event you need to break through. To do that, you need to spot a pattern from below or above, which requires a step-back skill.

A client once told me that she didn't benefit from her kinesiology session and that it didn't work for her. I understood why she said that and noticed that she no longer wanted what she asked for in the balancing session. The cost of what she needed to give up in order to get what she originally asked for was too high a price for her. She changed her mind after receiving what she asked me for, to not wanting it anymore because of the cost of what she needed to give up. To feel better about her decision to change her mind, she needed someone to blame and I became the scapegoat for something she could not take responsibility for. Since I was no longer contracted to continue working with her, I just smiled.

For my own growth, I needed to learn why she didn't shift through her problem. I now understand that each person, no matter what assistance is available to them, can only shift through a problem once they learn and understand the underlying spiritual lesson of the circumstances that surround the perceived problem. If they cannot spot the pattern, it will be repeated until the lesson is learnt. This lady could not move on because, even though she received the healing, her mind was still holding onto what she could not let go of. Each person has her or his own pace and time for change. Each time the circumstances that created the perceived problem are resolved, the person's soul will recreate the circumstances that started the problem in order to learn the spiritual lesson from them. This might seem strange, but in a way this lesson was mine to learn as a healer: each person has their own timeline and I have to respect that each person has their own experience of learning the spiritual lesson with a breakthrough.

What might appear to be a problem to you, might not appear that way to your partner. Until she sees the need to move beyond it, and ask the right questions from inside herself, she will not be able to break through it. I learned a great many lessons about breaking through problems from that experience and I will share some here.

Here I would like to make it clear that the timeline for your partner is not always the same as yours.

There is no way of anticipating time. The skill we need to acquire is to patiently wait for our loved one to find his or her way and let go of our expectations of them.

Taking responsibility for what is ours
Remember a key here is that our stuff is identified by the emotions we feel. So our frustrations are not necessarily directing us to blame our partners, but to recognise that those emotions belong to us as our stuff. The beliefs, meanings and expectations that hold them in place therefore also belong to us.

Now that we have inquired about what our stuff really is, we can deal with our own issues. We have also checked that our words are positive, in line with our outlook, and our focus is on the preferred outcome for our relationship. Now we hold space patiently for our partner to come around in her own time, at her own level of awareness.

Some people have less patience than others. Learn to cultivate patience as a virtue. What is reasonable depends on each person's nature and his or her willingness to grow.

By now we might recognise the ego saying, "I did it all right." Can you see what that might mean? What if we could exercise the same amount of patience with our partner, as we would want them to exercise with us? I wonder how many times the Creator runs out of patience with mankind? At what point did Jesus decide to make a whip and go and clean out the temple? The frustration of impatience stems from the anger we hold about not being welcomed into this world. Our inability to accept our partners just as they are is linked to our ability to bear witness as they grow into being their own people, already perfect.

To cultivate patience, letting go of anger will make way for acceptance and inner peace knowing that all is well in this world. It is this very letting go that shifts what we cannot control.

When we cannot break through

People often grow apart because they move in two different directions, according to their focus or values, or because one grows more quickly than the other.

In modern society, divorce is as easy as getting married. Women feel freer to exercise their will to divorce (accessing their inner masculine side) than to wait it out (embracing their inner feminine). It is true that when we change our circumstances, we are also more able to change our perspective. The separation we thought would bring the independence that protects us from experiencing pain, doesn't protect us from feeling the unconscious past pain, which is really what we're feeling through our current relationship mirror. Ironically, it is the very experience of separation that now becomes the push-through of a growth spurt that was inevitable.

Depending on the person's capacity to heal the hurt, they might even choose to go back to their previous partner who now also has a better understanding of their boundaries. If both partners grow, this deeper respect for boundaries allows the relationship to continue on another level. The new challenge is the capacity of both partners to open to each other and break down walls of previously held beliefs. If this is not possible because of self-preservation and a lack of understanding and compassion for one another's boundaries, the relationship is not sustainable.

Boundaries make relationships safe.

Our boundaries, and how we express them in our relationships, need to be addressed in every relationship and on each new level.

Healthy boundaries allow us to open to our partner fully so that breakthroughs can occur. When we know who we are, and we understand our own needs and values, it becomes a whole lot easier to be with someone else fully. If one partner's role is to express boundaries clearly, it is the other partner's role to respect them, rather than agree or disagree.

Find the overlap between boundaries as if they are two full circles and focus your attention on the overlap of the circles. In the overlapping gap you will find harmony and agreement in areas of commonality. Focus there as much as on your individual boundary needs, but respect them all. If you feel your partner is too focussed on her own boundary needs, you may struggle to relate.

Each person's internal pattern of how they make sense of information can be explained in terms of meta-coaching programmes, developed by Dr Michael Hall. Our behaviour identifies which patterns we commonly use to fill in information about the world. One particular meta-programme is referred to as sorting by other or self.

How do you relate to information you receive in business? Are you thinking, "What's in it for me?" Then you sort by self. Those who sort by other will label you as selfish if you sort by self. What is happening is that you are filtering information according to the way it serves you most of the time, but it also means that sometimes you forget to take other perspectives into account. Despite wearing the selfish label, you might still be exceptionally generous; this is just a selfish evaluation through someone else's filters. Those who sort by other put their own needs last. If you combine someone who sorts by other with someone who sorts by self the person who sorts by other is left feeling used. What is felt comes from inside us, and is no one's fault.

When opposites attract and one partner sorts by other and the other partner sorts by self are together, healthy boundaries to respect each other's approach are vital. Boundaries prevent feelings like being used because those feelings will be dealt with as he or she evolves. In reality, these two opposites do attract and this polarity plays out in relationships where the nurturer often sorts by other. From both sides, the perspective now might become that one is more focussed on a goal (masculine energy) and the other displays understanding and cooperation (feminine energy). Females can try acting on their feelings and males can be more understanding of female needs.

Of course, the male can also be feminine in nature and the female masculine. The original intention where both partners find their common ground by setting boundaries will direct a path for the relationship, like the banks of a river that contain and direct the flow. It is much easier to express needs openly to each other if we are connected with our hearts, and if we keep our eyes on the outcome we seek. Our awareness during these difficult times will be supported by a more positive experience as we journey together. With allowances for each other and not stating the obvious, which creates more focus on the obstacle, the solution will be visible to both parties when it appears. Although the solution is always present, we can only see it when we are ready and have moved past our own internal obstacles.

We need to focus on ourselves and not on our partner when seeking solutions. It is useful to remember that we are designed to self-heal and become more of ourselves and not to expect someone else to change.

Humans will always return to their nature, just like the scorpion that crossed the river on the frog's back. For the scorpion to cross the river he needed the frog's support. Before the scorpion stung the frog, he assured him he would not, because they would both drown crossing the river together. But he did it anyway as it was his nature. How can you be angry or impatient with nature? Always trust people, no matter how much they change, to go back to their nature.

Bees make honey; that is their purpose, but they don't have to understand it to do it. Understanding isn't a prerequisite to living our purpose, but it does help. It is vital to focus on yourself during times when you feel unhappy because your partner cannot break through an obstacle.

Your role here is to focus on yourself; to find the positive perspective in the situations when you struggle; to see the positive side and support your partner gently instead of appearing impatient. Often just a glimpse of hope is all they need.

Remember they can only notice the hope they need to break through when it is their time to see it. This is the fabric of real love. The type of love for a partner that gives us what we need on a laundry list is not *real* in this sense. It is not love at all, but an agreed exchange of needs.

The value of patience in breaking through

To be clever is great and to be patient is better. If we decide it is time to move on because we just cannot see a breakthrough, it is our own impatience and need to be right that motivates our behaviour. And upon that there is no judgement. If our nature does not allow us to wait patiently for our partner, the limitation is ours, as well as the free choice we exercise to move on. When we can make ourselves happy and still be held accountable for our own stuff, it is better than becoming negative. I taught my boys it is better to swear than to fight someone; the next step is to refine their expression from swearing to labelling emotion. In essence, we progress step by step.

We can lead a horse to water but the choice to drink belongs to the horse. If your partner chooses to stay focussed on the obstacle and cannot see the potential for hope, she will spiral in that frame until she understands the spiritual lesson. That does not mean she is lost to you. It just means you love her enough to give her the opportunity to find her own way. If you love something, set it free, right?

Hope doesn't give up

When it's dark all around you, the only way to know where to go is to look for the light. Hope, just a glimpse of it, might be enough if it's noticed at the right moment. There is always hope. Failure only happens when we give up. Surrender to a higher purpose – the obstacles on the way (our lack of vision to see the breakthrough) create who we become. This point is often the most crucial to building up to inner strength and eventually believing in yourself.

Sometimes the universe has a different plan in mind for you, and it was never up to you to choose your journey's milestones. But what is completely up to you is deciding how you choose to experience it.

Most times the very problem you face becomes the solution you seek. The question is, "Can you see it?" I love how Einstein said that problems could not be solved at the level they were created.

Have you noticed how when you stop looking for the solution it appears in its own time, and not a moment earlier? Notice how Einstein even knew we created the problem. Most empowering to know is that when we can see our role in it and admit it, we notice the change in perception. Name it and learn from it and all of a sudden what felt stuck starts to flow.

You have done all you could. Now you are done waiting. You notice your own part in the perceived problem.

Rock bottom is where it's at

You reach rock bottom. Only now will you create the turning point: when every bit of hope is shattered and you surrender, when you stop trying so hard to do it yourself. This moment of surrendering control made many writers famous today, because when they reached that rock-bottom place, their own lights went on inside. I have had moments like these when the answers just come to me. In these moments, the obstacles disappear and absolutely nothing can block the flow of energy that brings the solution with it. These are the breakthrough moments. In these moments we notice the solution that was often right there in front of us all the time. We had to stop trying, we had to surrender and admit that we didn't know. The moments that wisdom arrives are like lights in the dark that stand out so we can no longer see anything else. We make a complete new meaning of life and what appeared to us as a problem holds the key to the gift of life itself.

Your role as partner is to witness

In the relationship your role becomes that of witness when your partner experiences a problem that seems impossible for her to overcome. You can suggest solutions, but the best solutions will be the ones she finds herself, by searching inside. Any other external solution will only distract her for a while until she goes back to her self-inquiry process and self-reflection accesses the inner wisdom that will set her free. In fact, women experience such a deep internal struggle that they can hardly express what they need from you. What she needs practically during these moments more than anything else is to be heard by your heart.

She wants you to hear her without giving advice and she wishes for your complete mental presence in listening.

There are times when some of the issues she faces will appear to be impossible to break through. There are natural triggers during a partnership, like her loss of identity when she commits to a lifelong partner, has children, experiences menopause, realises she is ageing or becomes aware of death. With each physical experience comes a set of psychological aspects that she needs to work through unconsciously. A woman who experiences menopause has to deal with the knowledge that she can no longer physically birth life and needs to evolve her contribution in business or a new project to feed her need to nurture. This asks her to be beautiful and confident again, and possibly focus on her career. New and unknown, she experiences a brand new-personal identity process inside herself. Who is she if she cannot bear children anymore? What about her libido? Does her husband still see her as beautiful or will she succumb to an affair to feel like a young woman again?

Each psychological process has a spiritual lesson alongside it. Menopause asks a woman if she has matured her self-nurturing process. Does she love herself enough? Sometimes this is what drives her to be seen as beautiful so that she can be reminded of how to love herself again. Each process is part of human evolution, to assist us to know ourselves and grow into the potential of the lives we chose for ourselves.

Emotional sensitivity is a skill that can be learned if it doesn't come naturally to us. There are levels of maturity that can be applied to emotional intelligence levels:

- Infant – the need to know who we are
- Adolescent – learn trust
- Mature adult – to know others' needs before they do

Our emotional intelligence level is indicated by recognising if we, as a partner, still need to learn who we are, must learn to trust the process our partner experiences, or are mature enough to know what they need before they do.

Your partner needs to acknowledge her feeling to herself first. Everything is new to her. Once she has done that a few times, she can be encouraged to give it a name or describe it. It's the process itself that is valuable here if we want our partners to break through those tough internal struggles. Sometimes professional help is preferable, or your partner can speak to her girlfriends. However, the best person for her to open up to is you. The truth is that she needs *you*.

It's easier for you to see her stuff than it is for her

This is your opportunity to grow to the next level in your relationship. Your partner trusts you with her heart and wants you to witness her development, even if she doesn't realise it consciously. On countless occasions women sit in my office and share their feelings about their partners as they journey through their emotions and decide it's time to move on from their partner because they haven't grown with them through these times. I ask them if these are not words they need to share with their partner, and I encourage them to express it out loud. If you don't express it to the right person, with the right amount of energy, the result will be the beginning of a power play between two partners because it will create a wall that prevents intimacy because there are unexpressed emotions and thoughts at play.

Even if (and especially when) those words come slowly, that is when the work of transformation happens inside her. So patience here is truly a virtue. I understand that the uncomfortable feeling of sharing is the very energy that shows how vulnerable and naked she is when she is open. If men only understood what it requires to take even that small step, they might understand and start to feel how big the step of being willing to share and open up to her partner really is. There would be so many more couples together than separate if this could happen more often or more easily. In these moments there is only a glass of water. Now the partner who witnesses can also observe as she decides on her own that the glass is half full or half empty. These are the moments she really starts to take her power back, if you let her. These are the moments she will take responsibility for her own happiness and set you free from that burden. If you're impatient or show any sign of negative disapproval she cannot open for you. If you try to fix her she will stop and listen to you instead.

You'll feel good about helping her,
but her struggle will return and you'll ask again:
why can she not break through this?

Breakthroughs need vulnerability from her

The reward of a breakthrough is sweet, and those special times together will bind you. Events like weddings and funerals override any ambiguities in relationships between people, which is similar to the type of clarity you get from a breakthrough in a relationship, when she opens up to be vulnerable for you and you can nurture her. Notice how you can step into a nurturing role, which is you developing your own inner feminine.

There are moments when you know you need to express something but choose not to. Or in the opposite scenario, where an incident forces two people to deal with their stuff; the stuff they would ordinarily choose not to say, like after a tragic accident or out on the ocean in a confined space with other people. Nothing interfered with what they really wanted to share about their feelings for each other.

It's the same when we hit rock bottom in relationships. There seems to be nothing to lose of what we hold onto so desperately. We seem to be completely naked in each other's eyes and it feels as if in those moments the truth of it all allows us to fall in love all over again. The baggage is gone.

I remember years ago reading in John Gray's *Men are from Mars, Women are from Venus*, that as soon as we feel safe in a relationship we start projecting our baggage from our previous partner onto our current relationship partner. I also learned that this process never stops. The result is that we build huge walls between us. The sweet feeling of surrendering to our partner is left behind at the beginning of relationship, unless we make a conscientious effort to keep the walls around the two partners instead of between them. What we blame our partner for is ours. Because we are unable to see it, our partner reflects it to us with a higher intention so that we can break through those limiting perceptions and learn who we really are. The more we can accept ourselves, the more we can accept our partner. The truth is always beautiful, no matter how hard it seems at the time or how improbable the outcome.

When people shift apart, it's their
differences that separate them –
or rather the parts of themselves,
reflecting back at them,
that they cannot yet accept.

For her to be vulnerable she needs to feel safe

We can keep our minds open and our hearts loving if we're in a place of acceptance. From a place of fear, having to choose between what we think is right and what we think is wrong creates separation and keeps our focus and intention at that level of awareness without being able to access a suitable solution. Fear makes us focus on our partner's faults and prevents us from looking at ourselves. Just as the water and glass exist, we cannot deny the facts, nor should we. In a relationship situation, we should be able to separate the emotion from the event, which will allow us to see things for what they really are, instead of projecting. We can choose to see the glass half full if it serves us, or half empty, meaning we need to choose the appropriate meaning or find the positive intention that started the perceived difference in order to find a win-win solution.

My youngest son had an amazing karate grading at the age of seven. He skipped seven dinky belts and I asked him if he was scared. He said that he was scared but he didn't focus on it. We cannot deny that we feel fear, but we must learn not to focus on it. In a relationship, this means not choosing one partner as right and the other as wrong, but trusting the person we have selected and choosing the best outcome without wanting to change the other person. We all know inherently exactly what to do when the time comes. It's the distorted beliefs about how things should or should not be, that we have to unlearn. If we allow things to be as they are and refrain from making meaning from them, the energy will flow exactly where it should without us blocking it. Focus on your own happiness instead of focussing on your partner's obstacles. Notice if you would rather discuss your obstacles with your partner and invite her to do the same with you. If we can be there for each other, to use expression as a form of healing, it is a great gift in our relationship.

Compassion is the greatest emotional mastery any person can achieve. It only requires that you observe being fully mentally present and feeling with your partner without wanting to take their pain away.

Observation changes everything

There are stages of bonding in our relationships: sex, love and compassion. This shifts your awareness in levels from sex to love to compassion. Sex is physical bonding and will always close the circle that starts with a spiritual connection. Sex can also limit the level of awareness you reach without developing any further and can become a self-serving pursuit.

Love includes nurturing, affection and the appreciation that develops the emotional connection for a couple.

Compassion is the final level that merges with consciousness in a way that affects your partner through witnessing, without the need to influence or change her. There is wonderful research available now about mirroring in neuroscience that explains how it works when presence heals. Quantum physics explains the way waves (energy) form particles (solid matter) through the power of observing. When we stop looking at the waves, which appear as particles, the particles become waves again. We don't realise how powerful our attention is, because if we did we would be more aware of our intention when we pay attention.

This quality of mental presence is also explained when we distinguish doing-ness from being-ness as human beings. We just forget who we are. Conscious relationships are just another way to remind us that the quality of our relating and the desire to do so, are linked to expanding our experience of reality.

The only time we won't break through are when we are stuck in a negative spiral of feeling and thinking, at the same level that we experience the problem. Humans have 4000 concept thoughts from one day to the next. If we're lucky, 1% will be different from the day before. So we just keep running the same thought programs. Even the 1% we change from one day to the next depends on our ability to see a glimpse of a silver lining at the edge of the dark cloud.

All hope needs to stay visible so the answer is there when your partner is ready to see it. All you need is true love and a willingness to lead by example, not words.

I often wondered about my feedback skills to let my partner know what I could see from my perspective. The only times feedback ever worked was when he could see it in my behaviour or come to his own realisations. He could never really feel the intentions behind my words. My actions and my soft eyes invited him into my heart; those he can see, hear and touch. And then he could express to heal himself.

Questions

- What are the facts that you can see, hear, taste, touch and smell?
- Where exactly do you put most of your focus?
- Do you see the glass half full or half empty? Can you see just the glass of water before you decide if it is half full or half empty?

- Do you listen to the words you use in your conversations to explain what you're trying to say?
- How often do you recognise that what you say is really your stuff?
- Are you able to listen without showing approval or disapproval for your partner's expression of her struggle?
- How effective is your level of tolerance for your partner to find her own solution?

Chapter 9

Desire can be so cruel

Unconditional love is from above

It never fails to purify my soul I let you go

And my desire to be touched

For heart-love is always free

Here is my heart God

Wrapped in a red ribbon

May the one who opens it be gentle

– My Life Is the Love Letter

What If I'm Not Good Enough?

Traditionally a man offers a woman a certain way of life that she may have been accustomed to in her father's home. He makes this offer at the beginning of their journey together in exchange for her raising a family for them. He presents this lifestyle to her father. Man to man, they decide if it is good enough for her. Before any of that happens, the man has thoughts about himself, who he is, and what his purpose is in this world.

Deciding if we're good enough comes from the ego's need for purpose

Humans love to compare themselves to others to see how they fare. They count their accomplishments and decide their worth accordingly. Some people are stuck in the past, living the same pattern from when they had their highest achievements and keep repeating being that person. Others hope their ship will come in some time in the future. It's clear that the current way of doing things belongs largely to a system built on fear, and society has been designed for people to see themselves as separate from each other.

A relationship is no different; a relationship simply gives you someone to compare yourself to, through a lifetime and intimately. We compare ourselves to our partners and decide if we're good enough for one another. Sometimes, depending on various factors, we even believe we're better than our partners and feel dissatisfied with the exchange in the original agreement we made. We notice other potential partners around us. With a change in financial status, this is often very noticeable. Men start to cheat on their lifelong partners or reposition themselves in society without their partners.

This is where loyalty and betrayal become the separating extension tools that can follow on these experiences. Women feel as though they have also contributed to the family's financial status, by being the support structure, which enables the man to give his work his full attention, because that was the agreement they made. Others feel betrayed when their partners no longer see them as equal because they don't value their emotional investment in their home life. In the end, each man or woman decides for him or herself what their value is.

Often in codependent relationships the man or woman forgets who they were without their partner, which is why it's much healthier for each person to focus on their own happiness. Don't expect your partner to make you happy, but take responsibility for your own happiness.

I remember when I met my current partner. We went to a restaurant where they recognised him as a local celebrity. At first I was disappointed that the waiters addressed him before me. I felt surprised and maybe even ignored. For me this was an unusual experience and it created much unconscious competition between us. While in reality I matched him on most levels, I was clearly not as popular as he was because my work was done privately. For a long time in our relationship I would scold him for introducing himself as someone who worked for X in order for people to recognise him. This was my stuff and yet I projected it onto him.

During those times I didn't feel like I was good enough for him. Yet at no time did my partner ever say anything to create competition for attention. He is a very down-to-earth person and I loved him for the way he was when we were together. I just had a problem with the rest of the world for loving him that much as well. I wanted to consume his world so I did the one thing that many of us do when we reach this level of insecurity about ourselves. I tried to fill his world with me. I tried unconsciously to control him or his environment when I was with him.

Now, gentlemen, I'm sure you can think of times when you were flattered at first, but later felt trapped by ladies controlling you. Recognise this as their sense of inferiority at some level.

Using an example of someone else means that most of you will be able to see the symptoms of *not feeling good enough* quite clearly. Women appear clingy and try to place control outside of them when they cannot control what they feel inside of them. This is not just about ladies, but is the same for all of us. However, ladies do lose their radiance when this happens, as well as the attractiveness that magnetises masculine energy.

Our need to feel good enough is based completely on our sense of self-worth. When we don't feel good enough it is a signal that we're becoming unsure of who we are and we open the door to insecurity. This should be the alarm bell that tells us we're beginning to give our power away.

Can you recognise where you feel clingy with your partner? Do you notice when you're a bit controlling?

Once women are committed, what used to be pleasurable experiences become chores filled with expectations. To them it feels like men control their lives, their budgets, their freedom and every decision they make, whether this is true or not. Who would not feel trapped?

> *Unless our value is determined from inside us, someone else will always have a claim to our achievements and belief in ourselves before we truly understand that we were born good enough.*

Of course, we first wonder if we're good enough, before we know that we're good enough for our partners. Who told us how valuable we were? Was it our parents or our accomplishments? Were these events outside or inside us? Who holds the power over us? Is that why, when we feel inferior, we try to control others? Ironic, isn't it? What did we notice about our partners that made us think we are any less valuable than they were? Why do we even compare ourselves in the first place? Each person is unique – there is only one of you.

Your partner chose you because she felt something with you that no one before you had helped her feel about herself. Why be concerned about people your partner knew from long ago, when at any stage your partner could have chosen any of those people? Focus on yourself and notice who you gave power to, to decide how much you were worth.

You are priceless! You are truly one of a kind, through your thoughts and emotions. No one else is exactly like you. The feedback we receive from our partners is what truly allows us to see how much we still need to love and accept about ourselves. Next time you hear feedback that sounds like judgement, ask yourself if this is room for more value.

Who you are is enough

It always surprises me that my partner prefers me when I wake up in the morning with my messy hair, and loves my body with its curves, and yet I prefer to look groomed so I can show off my best.

How much more of myself do I still need to accept? We all have our expectations of what is required in a partner and what will make them good enough and equal to us.

A friend once told me that she chose her partner because of his straight teeth. Each person appreciates and notices something different, which influences their choice of partner. The only person who puts a label of good or bad on a personal characteristic is us, without really knowing whether this is a positive or negative for our partner. Each pot has a lid that fits, and our partners will teach us what we can still discover to love about ourselves.

Allow signs of not good enough to heal your stuff

When we wonder if we're good enough for our partners it has little to do with the relationship, and more to do with our relationship with ourselves. The chances are that the relationship will reflect some kind of internal abusive pattern. Yes, I know I need to be sensitive here, because the hardest part is admitting it.

If self-worth exists energetically, it also has to exist in our physical world in a story from our past or in unresolved issues, which play out what we experience inside. First we need to recognise that there is work to be done inside ourselves. And secondly, let's recognise that relationships are opportunities to heal this unresolved hurt from the past, even though it's not the objective. If we want to feel worthy for our partner, the process requires that we learn to love ourselves even more than we already do. I'm not referring to sorting by self as described in Chapter 7, but self value.

Can you recognise where in the past you decided how to think of yourself? Maybe someone said you did a splendid job or that what you did wasn't good enough and that determined your sense of self as you value it. It's important here to consider that the words we remember aren't necessarily the truth, but our interpretation of what happened. My sister and I grew up in the same bedroom and we had completely different childhoods – one was happy and one was unfortunate. For now, just observe where you have emotions about your achievements, or a lack thereof. This will allow you to make a new meaning. When we are grown up, we understand that what someone might have said in the heat of the moment is not about us at all.

A client of mine was left behind with a neighbour when she was very young so her mother could tend to an emergency. This tiny little girl decided that she was not good enough to get her mom's attention. Once she remembered the incident as an adult, she realised that the meaning she made about her value was not true. Her mom just had to go to hospital, but did care enough to leave her in the care of the lovely neighbour. Kids don't have all the information at the time and they make meanings about who they are through their parents' eyes as best they can. These meanings become what they believe about themselves when they grow up, and that is what we come to believe as our truth, even if it's not really the whole truth.

Getting to know ourselves is such a wonderful discovery in our relationships. When we wonder if we're good enough, our partners are often best suited to give us feedback to reflect on and consistently increase our sense of self-worth. Think of it as a game, and notice when you compare yourself, that you come from a place of separation and fear, not love. Love is inclusive and kind. Fear is judgemental and competitive; it separates us from each other when all we do is reflect to each other what we can accept or resist about ourselves in the moment. In fact, to feel good about ourselves and increase our self-worth (when it is based on fear) means that we have to let someone else look bad in order for us to look better, making one value more important than another.

Your partner loves you just as you are. How you feel can give you information about the higher values you have not yet discovered in yourself.

A partner who told you that you are not worthy is secretly afraid that they are not as good as you. They compare, and by not defending yourself, you allow them to see how silly their words are. They cannot play this game with you if you are not a willing participant. In time, love will conquer all.

I got anxiety attacks in my car after experiencing two smash-and-grab incidents in two months. I had to learn coping skills quickly and I decided to try to convert the fear I felt to love; I decided to smile at people walking up to my car. In South Africa, we have many beggars and hawkers on the roads at traffic lights. I looked them in the eye and smiled as best as I could, and filled my heart with love for them. To my surprise, most people didn't handle this energy well and would walk away fast. Maybe the behaviour was unfamiliar to them. Others smiled back and I knew that at least for that person, I brought a little sunlight, even though I wasn't willing to open my window. There was some form of acceptance that set in. I realised that when something or someone's agenda was from a fear-based consciousness, they could not tolerate to be in that space of love and left me very quickly. Five years later I had no more incidents with my car and my anxiety went away.

Questions

- Who told you what you are worth?
- Do they deserve to have that power over you, or would you like to take it back?
- Write down what you are worth.
- How can you learn what you are worth from your relationship?
- How can you increase your value when you become aware of your insecurity?

Chapter 10

An angel vision of hell

Suppressed soul in chains

Break free from your sleep

Remember the love we had

Feel it in your bones

Dance to the music

Complete me forever

Come here no more

My only battle be love

– Lonely Heart

Feeling Alone Inside The Relationship

The feeling of loss is one of the saddest emotions. I believe that deep in the psyche is the sense of being separated from our creator. Do you like pictures of landscapes, and of open spaces? If you do, they talk to a place deep in your subconscious where you recognise flat lands stretching out far in front of you because this was the mental imprint you received when humankind was first created.

The first understanding of feeling separate
When babies are between the ages of six and 18 months they realise that they are not part of their mommy anymore. We teach them to play peek-a-boo from a young age. They begin to grasp that they are separate from mommy. Peek-a-boo (hiding behind a cloth so they cannot see us and then reappearing) teaches them that mommy will come back again. As they spend time apart from mom when they need her, they realise that mom is not always there. In a baby's mind there is only now. A baby only engages with what is in front of it. In time, baby realises that mom doesn't always help with the needs of hunger when she's called. Baby starts to develop a sense of time and memory and that it is separate from mom, and feels alone. This phenomenon can also be called

separation anxiety. The big unknown world waits for baby. Even at such a young age the need for identity starts to develop. A little baby knows himself through his mom. Baby will start to learn who he is through the people he or she encounters, each time getting to know him- or herself a little bit better. The pattern for relating in order to know yourself is set.

Transferring bonding from family to partner

Relationships are the same in the sense that a bond is created. A woman will leave her parents behind to enter into a marriage with her new partner. The process of knowing herself through her family is now becoming a process of getting to know herself through her partner and her own children. Until we discover we aren't known just through our partners and that there is more to us, this remains the extent of our awareness.

I have known myself mostly through relationships. In that way, who I believe I am is mostly through the eyes of the men I have been with. For many people this experience of recognising themselves can also be rooted in belief systems like religious organisations.

Finding ourselves again by searching for God

Many of us embark on a journey of getting to know ourselves without partners, or friends, or any human beings. I'm going to call it spirituality for now. Have you ever heard someone say they are spiritual but not religious, or wondered why people spend hours sitting in meditation?

When this journey to the self starts, we experience a fair amount of what I am going to refer to as separation anxiety, or a sense of loneliness.

At this stage people are insecure and lost, and notice chaos around them. If not perceived through the eyes of other people, they don't quite know where they belong and little makes sense to them through this *lens*. This can be dangerous since the search itself requires that we let go of who we thought we were, yet subconsciously we still need something to hold onto. I suppose this is the time that people find cults or other groups for that sense of belonging. Jung calls it the process of individuation. And some teachers say that you become insane before you come to your senses. The benefit of going through this experience is that you discover who you are without looking through other people's eyes.

In the process you learn how to evaluate and tell truth from perception. Everything is seen for the first time. The rules we once knew don't work here and everything looks upside down like it did for Alice in Wonderland. Thomas Moore, who was a monk for ten years before he became a psychotherapist, explains this searching in his book *Dark Nights of the Soul*. As I mentioned before, I too travelled on vision quests in Peru and Hawaii to "find myself".

Even weirder is what I will tell you now. At some point in my spiritual evolution my mentor told me about facing my shadow. I used to think a shadow was an evil and dark thing and what he said made me cringe. But I knew that I wouldn't consider his words if I wasn't ready for it. So I asked him how I could face my shadow. After I did what he suggested I found myself in a dream where I felt a pain *so big* inside me that I recognised it as my shadow. Because I asked consciously to see my shadow, I knew exactly what the feeling was. I expected to find out about some bad thing I did in my past or another lifetime, but that was nowhere near the torment I felt from my very first separation from Source.

I knew that this deep, sad feeling came from my disconnected sense of what most people experience as God.

What does all this spirituality have to do with the experience of separation anxiety in relationships? Firstly, if we still experience ourselves through our partner's eyes, rather than through our own eyes, we're at risk of experiencing heavy bouts of feeling lonely every time we let go of a little of their view of us in order to make space for our view of ourselves.

Each rejection creates a feeling of separation anxiety at first

When we bond with a mate in a relationship, there is also a disconnection that occurs as we let go of the expectation of what we want our partners to be, projected through our eyes. Indirectly we shift our sense of identity from the feedback they give us to the meaning we make for ourselves of who we are.

Every time there is a sense of separation because we don't expect something on our laundry list to be provided by our partner, we disconnect a little and let go of expectations.

Experience can also occur just on an emotional or energetic level, and present the same real experience in the mind as this disconnection. Every time something happens, whether we just expect it or it actually happens, the experience of it in our minds is as if it is real.

When the relationship is conscious we agree to work openly with what we think and feel. These experiences can indicate a self-inquiry into codependence with one partner or both.

It took me a long time to realise that these feelings of separation anxiety are not an indicator of a codependent relationship, but rather a reflection of disconnection in purpose between two people. When there is a codependence, you can't see how you can live apart from the other. When you experience separation anxiety, there is a feeling of loneliness. The process of knowing ourselves is a journey we embark on alone.

Every time we feel lonely we can accept more of the love we are

Until we know who we are, our quality of sharing with another is limited. We either show ourselves as a reflection of ourselves or we show up as ourselves. Once I was given the vision of a Buddha's reflection on the water and the comparative actual Buddha's statue above the water (read to me during a balance from Gregg Braden's *The Divine Matrix*). I was shown that all I could see from my perspective was the reflection in the water. In a relationship, this would be the partner's feedback to us of who we are as a reflection of the actual statue in the water. If we know the self truly, we'll focus on the physical Buddha's statue and it will appear that much clearer.

When we're alone a mate doesn't provide an outside reflection of an inner world – that is something we have to find on our own.

The journey of the dark night of the soul is how we learn who we are, without people telling us.

We need to go inside and there are many ways to do it. When we enter a relationship from this space, we see things differently and we bring all of us to the relationship. Our partners are still a soundboard, but the dialogue within happens at the same time. Before we are fully known to ourselves, feeling separate is as much part of the relationship as anything else.

There is also a sense of two equal partners who are separate for the time being. Maybe this is experienced more often at the beginning of a relationship. A person who knows who he or she is, is also aware of their connection to God Source. Love is relating and, as individuals, we relate first to God and then to our partners. You can imagine how this could impact on the quality of the relationship. What some people perceive as strange, may be understood better by others who are comfortable with their sense of self. For example, the need to spend time alone or in meditation can also be referred to as a need for self-inquiry. People ask why we are here and if you believe it is to experience yourself as awareness, you understand the value of taking time to get know yourself without reflecting yourself through other people's beliefs and values. The clearest way to know yourself is to see yourself. Some people ask me why we meditate and how do we do it. Notice how we've forgotten how to just be and need to read books like *A New Earth* to bring us back to the present moment. I too have tried many ways to meditate, but I find the most useful to be the times when I float between here and there. I can observe many things and still be grounded enough to bring back to memory how what I see might apply. Because we have to eat and sustain our bodies, the practice of learning about and respecting our bodies is as important as learning all about ourselves. Interacting with people helps us to be present and become grounded through engaging so we can see ourselves through their eyes. Light in the light cannot see anything.

Don't mistake being alone for rejection

If we take time out in quiet meditation to clear our minds from what is happening in our environment, our vision of what is going on becomes clearer, as does our perception of who we are and who our partner really is. A certain amount of alone time is needed if we wish to maintain a co-creative relationship. But this can be misunderstood by some partners as rejection and partners can experience a form of disconnect from their partners with anxiety, until we realise that connecting to ourselves is healthy for a co-creative relationship. Our partner always comes back after doing what is necessary. Trying to hold onto her will keep her from developing a deeper relationship with herself, without which your relationship risks developing a form of codependence. Don't use this alone time as an excuse to disconnect from your partner and to connect with your mates. Alone time is exactly that – time for the self to hear that still inner voice and know thyself.

Each time we experience these emotions they invite us to define who we are without the other, and make complete space inside to connect upwards instead of sideways. Each time a partner wishes to be alone to find themselves is an opportunity to hold space for them or for them to do the same for us. Feeling rejected closes our hearts and cuts us off from our partners. Naturally, people's needs to experience this will differ, depending on their soul evolution. Each person has his or her own rhythm. Until the time arrives and the relationship is experienced in an integrated way where apparent rejection is received with a smile, what is inside is experienced as the same as what is outside of us. Disconnecting is as much a skill as engaging fully mentally with our partners.

At the beginning, the frequency of our partner is so amazing that we cannot get enough of it when we find them. Doing stuff together all the time also creates a build-up to healthy time apart. Remember creation is a process of connecting and pulling apart towards personal freedom. The test is to ask when we are together: are we the same person as when we are apart? When we aren't physically with our partner, can they still feel us inside? Do we know their state of being, as the mental connection between us develops?

Conclusion

Experiencing being alone in relationships is healthy to maintain the balance that prevents codependent relationships. The need to be alone is neither meant to create anxiety in our partners nor to be used as an escape to disconnect from our partner's neediness. Being alone has value for the journey of the soul's evolution to reconnect with itself to propel us forward with the purpose that moves our relationships forward. Being alone is as natural as intimacy when we bond. The freedom it brings takes our connection to a new level where we discover more of ourselves to relate with and experience love.

The conditioned development of human beings leaves us feeling insecure and without a sense of belonging until we can connect within with a sense of self. This gives us the confidence to live from within, with an internal frame of reference and emotionally free from outside influence, trusting our own intuition. The value of being alone reflects through our search for our creator in the dark night of the soul. Here we meet our sadness when we realise it is we who see ourselves as separate and we reconnect, not only to who we really are but also to our partner.

Every time we feel rejected we discover more of us to reconnect and this allows us to accept more of ourselves as we also encounter this in our partner. We need time alone and this is no reflection on our love for our partner.

Chapter 11

Smell the fumes of confusion

That sting inside

Leaving imprints of growth

– How Deep Is Your Love?

The Impact Of Attachment

A word probably best known in Buddhist circles, referred to as attachment, is the reason for all suffering. It came to me in a different way.

The first time I actually heard the word, it was a feeling. I had a dream before a significant event I will not share here. Just before I woke up at 3 am, I dreamt about a place where water had the texture of liquid metal. The colour was the same as water but it was thick in consistency, the kind of thick texture that would explain how shapes could form and come out of it. In the dream, I was standing near the plasma-water. The shapes coming out of it were like hands and the hands were beckoning to me. They wanted something from me. Whatever they wanted I gave, but I cannot recall what that was. I gave what they wanted, and they wanted more. Now more hands appeared. I gave again. And the more I gave, the more they seemed to want – it was almost like greed. All of a sudden I felt repelled by the hands and removed myself from them.

Attachments bounce off safe boundaries

In general I enjoy giving. I even consider myself a rather generous person. Since having the dream I can distinguish one's energy from another as if I could feel the intention of someone's asking. Within myself I felt freedom. My experience of people was not necessarily that they had that inner freedom. Since the dream, when someone wants something from me, I have always been able to sense if that underlying attaching energy was present or not.

Giving without expecting something releases attachment

I've learned that there are two ways to give: I can give from love without expecting anything back or I can give expecting something in return. For a long time in my life I tried to understand the energy of things like money. I have come to learn that attachment or receiving without being satisfied and grateful is closely linked to the way humans interact with each other.

People will ask you for help, and you are free to assist them or not. If they expect assistance, it is a form of attaching to you to keep rescuing them when they're in trouble. It reminds me of the saying that one should teach a man to fish rather than give him a fish. If someone asks from need and you give because you can and it gives you joy without expecting anything back, it also prevents any form from attaching to you.

Name the attachment to bring it out of hiding

If one chooses to assist and wishes to invite the victim to let go of his attachment, it is important to address the attachment. Jesus did this when he spoke to the spirits in men to go into the pigs.

Attachments are like parasites. They need willing participants whose life force they can drain. I don't know why they've chosen a path to feed off other humans, but that is where each form of consciousness is in its soul's evolution. Maybe someone who chooses to cut off from their own life force needs others' energy to sustain themselves.

Why we need to understand attachments in relationships

The reason for addressing attachment in the context of conscious relationships, and male and female roles, is that there are certain games that women play. Somehow women are vulnerable to this attachment energy from eons of collective projections, as victims who have been violated. Our bodies, being physically weaker than men's, require that we be internally stronger. I remember my mother telling me when I was small that if I'm not stronger, I need to be smarter than men. Women are also naturally more emotionally intelligent and we develop better communication skills.

When you combine that with our early female experiences of giving life, it's a potent combination. The earliest power experience is when a woman starts to bleed and realises that she can have babies. A man still has to prove his strength before she will notice him. Instead of beauty from the heart, this is replaced by the games women play. The potent combination of emotional manipulation and using sex becomes the foundation for a distortion of what love might actually become in her mind.

How we give permission for attachment

Power replaces love, sex replaces beautiful radiance, and service to self overrides the collaborative win-win outlook needed for a healthy relationship.

We give attachments permission in our lives as soon as we want more than we really need. A hole in our boundary is all that is needed to exploit any form of vulnerability and justify a belief like survival of the fittest. I remember in the corporate world how much I valued a smart move, even when my opponent in trading had taken the risk that took me out, because he was clever enough to think of it. Only later in my career did I empathise with blue-collar workers who lost their ability to feed their kids because of business decisions I had a part in, like when South Africa's textile industry was handed on a plate to China. Just because it serves us in the short term doesn't mean it is the right action.

I've learned that firm and clear boundaries can increase the chances of a win-win solution in relationships even when there's a power struggle. Boundaries ensure sufficient energy to make exchanges equal, rather than leaking energy that attachments can feed off. The most important reason I address a deep spiritual aspect like attachment is because codependent relationships are fertile ground for cultivating mutual attachment to each other. Visually, relationships can look like cords attaching to two people where they feed off each other.

Replace attachment with conscious bonding
To be in a conscious relationship where we are truly free and connect with intimacy to share source energy together in love and joy, we grow in our intimacy as we let go of our attachments to each other. I'm not sure if freedom can exist inside a relationship without the attachments that are represented by expectations.

It also has that needy energy that always wants more of us. I never understood why men who experienced my radiance fell in love with me. Of course, what they really fell in love with was their own image reflected to them by the inner work I did and my ability to be a clean mirror for them. On my part, I never understood why I didn't feel what they did until I understood the needy energy of attachment. I just didn't resonate with it at all. Although I felt love for them and my heart was open, it wasn't physical for me at all. It might seem odd that I get married so easily again and again, and I have never been single for more than a few weeks, but when I found I resonated with these men in my life, I either had a once-off experience with them or I married. I consider my once-off experiences healing experiences. Each time I loved with all that I could, but just not with that energy of attachment. In the dream, it was as if all the hands and the water were all part of the same water entity and whatever I gave them disappeared into that shape as soon as they received what I gave, leaving them always empty-handed.

Cutting cords of attachment strengthens conscious relationships

The separation anxiety experienced in a relationship is when fear sets in that one partner might leave. The fear comes from the energetic cords that attach a couple being cut off, severing access to life force from one person to another. I used to think that it was people who attached themselves because they didn't do the work of connecting to their own inner life force, but later I realised that we give our power away by the mere act of not trusting ourselves. When we start to believe what other people tell us about how the world works or believe in something more than we believe in ourselves, we give our power to that belief, thing or symbol. These beliefs, things or symbols are given energy to exist in what Rupert Sheldrake identified as morphogenic fields. I had an inner experience once where I saw formless, brownish mist. Inside it, I heard talking about what could have been science. Maybe this is an energy thought form that is man-made, that is part of what enables our world to exist. What was it? Where did it come from? All I knew was I was in it, but not part of it at all. I didn't know why I was there. Maybe it was to talk about it here now and to understand more about a type of attachment. I remember thinking in the experience that the voices I heard speaking to each other didn't even know I was there, as if I was just observing the situation.

Get energy from your inner source rather than through exchanging energy

People who are connected to their own inner source and who walk as lights are targets for others who want to attach and feed. Energy that needs to attach to another energy source to sustain itself can drain our resources. Just like we can choose to sustain ourselves, instead of expecting someone else to take care of us, it's our responsibility not to encourage attachment-like energies to feed off our life force. Feeling sorry for someone is not being responsible with our own energy. My late husband used to say, "Fuck the people; we are the people." Energy starts at home – we feed a poverty consciousness when we try to save people. People need to learn to save themselves. Show them how to help themselves with skills and give what is ours to give freely. They choose to learn or not. If any sinister form of energy attracted to the other person has a right to exist in our world made up of sound and light, it becomes its own host and connects to its own creator or leaves us. You have a responsibility to have a relationship with yourself and what you consider your creator, rather than rely on your partner for inspiration and fulfilment of your needs.

Relationships are hard enough – be aware of what you allow to drain your energy. We have a responsibility for what we have been given. In the Bible there is a lesson about the talents people are given. They are not asked to compare them, only to show how they invested them. This is our responsibility in relationships too. How are we doing with what we were given by nature?

In our bodies our feelings are the closest access we have to the physical experience of sound. Think of those times when something went wrong and you didn't trust your gut feeling, only to regret it later. Act on what you feel rather than rely on logic (which is made of light). There are moments in the soul's evolution when the wisdom not to follow logic or rules overrides courage. One example would be in a battle where hundreds of brave men go up against thousands of stronger men – is it wiser to stay or to go? If you know the real reason the order was given, which will result in hundreds of good men being sacrificed, will you do as you are instructed? Are you wise enough not to follow the rules for the right reason? That marks a turning point in a soul's evolution. To do it one would need a stronger inner source from which to draw energy than those whose orders you follow. Can you recognise your inner voice and believe in yourself? Believing in your partner and trusting her will follow.

The real purpose of attachment is to imprison our minds from observing all that is there

Maybe the Buddhists are right about attachment being the reason for all struggling; I've just never been able to understand it from a knowledge point of view. Be very aware in your relationship of when you don't feel completely free to be yourself. Let freedom guide you. I live from my heart, even when I don't really know who or what God is. Yet it hasn't become a requirement for me to dialogue with this universal power, which is always there. If he doesn't want me to limit myself in my own mind, why should I limit who he is?

Always ask your partner for what you need, without expecting her to say yes, and be prepared to accept no. This will leave you both free from attaching to each other.

Conclusion

Always recognise your sense of free will to say no when asked for something by your partner. If you feel obliged to assist, notice where you are projecting a need to rescue her inside yourself. The impact of helping from this place allows dependence to creep subtly into your relationship. There is always joy in the ability to share from a free place inside you because you're doing something that comes quite naturally. In the event that you have to ask for help, first notice if you can do this for yourself. Remember, when you ask your partner that she is completely free to answer yes or no. Fully accept the answer you receive as it will reflect your reverence for their values rather than expect their help.

Attracting attachment is natural when we don't know ourselves fully as we *take on* the projections others encourage us to believe about ourselves. Become aware of how you feel when people ask you for favours and you'll recognise your own inner knowing of people's intentions, even when they're unaware of it.

The less attachment you allow in your relationships the stronger the conscious bond, because both partners choose to be there from a free place inside themselves.

Chapter 12

༄ What is behind the mask

That you choose to show the world?

Or do you have a different colour mask

For every person you meet?

Do you use it to interface

Between what you really feel

And what you want to say?

What if you take the mask away?

Come with me

I show you me as I really am

And you me you as you really are

What happens when two hearts merge? ༄

– A Poem with No Name

Too Close For Comfort

A partnership implies a connection, which could become too close depending on our ability to know ourselves.

During the development of a relationship we often encounter red flags. We ask if we are too close for comfort, "Should I tell her at this moment about a previous sexual experience?" Or "Should I let her know my financial situation?" There are many situations that warrant openness but for reasons of self-preservation we prefer to say the minimum and keep our partners on a need-to-know basis.

How much honesty is too much?

We've mentioned how conscious relationships require honesty and transparency to prevent walls between us. You are both individuals and you create your own experiences of happiness without expecting your partner to do it for you. We've expressed our boundaries in terms of our nature and we have a strong sense of who we are to each other, with few expectations. What harm can there be in being too open?

How much talking is necessary?

Some people talk too much and many of them are female. She doesn't realise that her partner being a good listener doesn't give her a license to have verbal diarrhoea because she loves an audience.

What people don't realise is that their words reflect their values and beliefs. If you ask them to tell you what they value, you'll probably encounter a blank look. A good coach can easily use a process called Neuro-Linguistic Programming (NLP) to establish what someone really believes behind the mask of the words they use to talk about themselves. NLP is so powerful that some states in America banned it from being used. What people don't understand can often be mistaken for magic of some kind.

As ancient wisdom goes, "Say what is kind, what is true, what you have learned first-hand, and only when it is necessary."

Speaking for closeness

What we don't yet realise is that we speak because we need to hear ourselves say things in order to absorb them. It is almost as if the words come from the unconscious mind talking to the person. Our words are hardly ever spoken for the benefit of the external listener, even when we think we are saying them for him or her. Our words reflect, in that moment, who we are. Therefore we need to notice our own words and the place from which they're spoken. It's useful to notice what our intention is for speaking in the first place.

If my partner is wonderful I want to share more of myself with him. I speak a lot because I love myself. Many of the words I speak might create resistance in my partner as he'll have a different view on a topic or those words may even build walls between us. Of course, this doesn't happen consciously, but in the background my partner gets to know more about me. Each word is a reflection that allows him to decide if he has accepted that part of himself, which is alive and well in me. You can imagine how much sharing can create a sense of yourself, both the parts you like and the parts you dislike.

Listening invites close reflection

A colleague of mine used to say very little about herself at the office. She was a wise soul and moved her way up to take a leadership role later. No one really knew her. Most people liked her because she just listened and hardly ever expressed how she felt, which would, by default, create a resistance in other people towards her. I never got close to her because if she didn't share neither did I, as I am a natural introvert. She kept to herself and that was how she maintained the distance she needed to not have to reveal herself through expression.

Notice how much this taught you about me. I express a story explaining my behaviour all the time. Now you know I'm an introvert, and that I value listening as a skill to be successful. What was my purpose for sharing the story? To show you how many ways there are of sharing.

Intimacy provides the closest reflections

Let me tell you a story of a little boy who tells his mommy that he is leaving home. His mom packs his bag and gives him a sandwich for lunch on his journey that day. His first stop is the park. There is an old lady sitting on a bench. He joins her and the birds that surround her. By lunchtime he gets hungry and shares his sandwich with her. She feeds the pigeons too and smiles at him. He smiles back. When it gets dark he decides to go back home. His mom asks him about his adventure and he says that he met God. "God was an old woman," he said. "She never spoke, but she smiled and fed the birds."

In another part of town the old lady returns to her son's home. When asked about her day she says that she met God. It was a beautiful boy who smiled at her and gave her a sandwich.

Words or no words, we communicate in so many ways. How much we communicate doesn't depend on what we choose to say or its relevance, but clearly on the receiver's frame of mind and depth of perception. In each case, the boy or the old lady reflected to each other a part of themselves they perceived as God, whatever that was to them.

The wall of not sharing pushes us away

If we wonder about the need to keep our symbolic wetsuits on with our partners, there is no right or wrong answer. The situation and the necessity will determine how much transparency is required in the moment. Our partners will feel the intention behind our communication. If we choose not to tell because we want to keep that part safe just for us, our partner will feel an invisible wall growing between us. If we share words that don't come from kindness, we are putting something into the field between us that will come back later for healing.

Intuition teaches us how much closeness we need

The more sensitive we are, the more we will be aware of thoughts and feelings that may or may not be ours. When we're connected to our higher sense of self, we notice lots of feelings and thoughts around us. Some environments even feel different to others. When I was in Cusco, Peru it felt different to Johannesburg, South Africa. The thoughts around me were different. People drive differently on the roads. The thoughts we attract are not that different to what we hold in our fields, based on who we believe we are. If we have a thought about a previous sexual experience with another partner while we're with our partner in an intimate situation, we can ask ourselves what that thought is doing there. Is it because we need to express it? For whom are we expressing it – for our partner's benefit or for our own healing? Will it be relevant or kind to express it now? What will happen if we choose to share it now? Or do we just notice it and let it float through our minds? Was it triggered by something in our environment but doesn't really belong to the moment? Do we know our partner well enough to share it? Whatever our highest potential is, is where we should go with this.

Creating closeness consciously and safely

The wisdom to make our own rules, in the moment, lies in knowing that everything we say *does express how we choose to create ourselves*. Even the thoughts we have create who we are when we focus on them. And the more we focus on them the more our partner will feel them too.

We start having experiences in our relationships where our partners use the intimate information we share with them against us. This leaves us with an internal question next time of whether we want to express with them openly, and the question is: How dangerous is it to share the information with our partner? The danger in being too close for comfort is that you question what is safe to share with your partner and how you choose to share what you feel. What you need to understand is that you need to create a safe environment in which she can share with you; you need to understand the impact of using the information you found out about when she was vulnerable, in an argument.

There will be times we don't want to open up to our partner because we got burnt, especially after a divorce or past painful experience. This is difficult and it can take time before we feel beautiful enough to open again. Know that we filter out the experience of love if we choose to remain closed – not just closed to love but also closed to getting to know more about ourselves. If we take responsibility for our own happiness and understand that respectful sharing needs mindfulness too, we can express ourselves inside our relationships as creatively as we wish. Expression is joyful. What is more fun than being seen? To be heard, as long as we are prepared to give our partners an equal opportunity at the time they request to be heard, as they discover their own potential.

> *The only things holding us back are our own fears and limits of perception because of what we need to heal.*

Can you love with abandon, inside and out? Even pain is myth if you really want to know. In my past separation experiences, I have been surprised at my partners' ways of self-preservation when I loved with abandon. But I dusted myself off and carried on because if I chose to hold onto that, it would always cloud my judgement and I'm no longer in that experience. A successful marriage is one where forgiveness is the most refined skill.

Share to connect for freedom

The better you can express your need in the moment, rather than finding someone to blame (because an emotion is not healing) the more you will live in freedom. Relationships are not meant to trap us in just another belief system. They are opportunities to share who we are with someone who cares to know. Why remain with someone who doesn't give you the same level of attention that you're willing to give him or her?

A woman has a need to connect and a man has a need to be free, or so the myth goes. The truth is that if she wants to connect consciously, she unconsciously wants to be free, and the opposite for the masculine energy. In a relationship, the feminine will attract masculine free energy to her with her beauty. He will open her and they will both be satisfied and be free again. There is a pattern here of an open and closed flower, repeating the experience. As long as the flower has sweet pollen, the bee will keep returning when the sun's rays open the flower. If the bee stays too long, the sunset will close the flower and the flower petals trap him inside. The flower needs to make more pollen and the bee needs to make honey. This movement is what creates life itself.

Close comfort is sweet but not necessary all the time. With each close connection each partner learns more about him- or herself and integrates this into their identity. With each encounter the connection can be deeper and move from separation into freedom and be freer than before expanding the created experience together. Remember the connection and desire it again, and repeat the process from connecting to freedom and being freer so you connect more deeply every time.

Conclusion

- Recognise that we are too close when we see ourselves more through our partner's eyes than our own.
- Knowing ourselves means we're never left insecure about how information we share might threaten how we see ourselves.
- Honest expression leaves no room for the misunderstanding of assumptions.
- Saying a lot is only wise if we know when sharing it will serve the relationship.
- Sharing teaches us that our internal reality is different to our partner's and we each have our own experience of reality.
- Sharing allows us to have compassion for each other's map of how the world works.
- We say what we need to hear since we are the ones to benefit most from our own advice, instead of being concerned with impressing our partner.
- Maybe we can learn to listen with the intention of understanding values and boundaries, instead of replying and growing our relatedness as we decide before the time, if we say too much.

- Our reactions, with or without emotions, always provide mirrors for our partners, and for them it's always close. Taking feedback personally is taking the risk of feeling too close. We cannot really affect this for our partners, we can only experience this for ourselves. If we feel too close, notice what message lies behind the mirror our partner provides for us.
- When pain closes you, ask the question – am I too close?
- The closeness of intimacy is not just what we desire, but also what we fear. Be careful what you wish for, you might just get it. Will you be ready when you do?

Chapter 13

The call to be complete

To be heard and understood

To be free from expectation

And connected to love

– When I Write

How Do I Maintain My Freedom?

As mentioned in the previous chapter, the process of connecting and breaking free is how we create. When we can no longer let go to be free inside ourselves, our identities become intertwined. Of course, every relationship will have its own couple's magic, but inside, it needs to consist of two complete individuals and not two halves. When a person no longer knows who they are without the other, a codependence has formed.

Take responsibility for your own happiness to be free

A healthy intimate bond is free from expectations that our partner can make us happy or sad. Like anything, it starts inside us and depends on how prepared we are to be free. Do we prefer to be accommodating about it or will we notice consciously when we reach the edges of the boundaries where we are no longer prepared to grow?

Maintaining freedom is a function of free will. Every human being has this basic right and our level of freedom depends on our level of awareness to recognise the truth.

Freedom means we don't judge

Free will allows each one of us to have our own opinions without judgement. If we want to stop ourselves from falling into the trap of being in any kind of codependent relationship, we need to allow our partners to have their own viewpoints, without deciding if they are right or wrong. This will help us to maintain our independence and live co-creatively in freedom with each other, free from what might have happened to us in the past.

Knowing ourselves is the foundation for freedom

Love is a resonant frequency or, as I put it before, all-inclusive. That means that love does not disagree. When we disagree, we cannot experience true love. If our wish is that our partner always agrees with us because we want to be right, that's not love either. This is a need for attachment and it comes from the ego, because we still struggle to see ourselves unless we look through our partner's reflection. Disagreement comes from deciding the glass is half full or half empty instead of seeing simply the glass of water, without having an opinion about it. Or having an opinion about it, but not expecting our partner to agree with it. Disagreeing means we made a judgement call that expresses us in the moment. When we pull back our projection and just observe the facts with soft eyes we renew our foundation for freedom, allowing our partner to express differently and let it be alright.

Learning freedom from ancient wisdom

Maintain your freedom by applying Toltec wisdom:
- Be mindful with your words. Communicate clear messages that are relevant and requested. Speak your truth from love. Say what the facts are as you interpret them.
- Don't take what your partner says personally. Recognise that she might be expressing what she needs to hear right now, projecting from her internal reality.

- Don't assume anything by making your own meanings. Rather ask questions that will reveal what she really means and listen with love, and then state how you disagree. Try to see the glass of water and ask your partner if they see the glass to find common ground.
- Just do the best you can. Don't beat yourself up for mistakes, and let them go too. Accept that your best is good enough.

Love yourself to free yourself from neediness
Use every opportunity to learn to love yourself more. Free up as much energy as you can to allow the experience to show yourself in the purest light, free from heavy emotions that keep you from flowing and knowing who you truly are.

Be conscious of accountability
I have come to know that there are certain responsibilities that have to be adopted in order to master freedom in a conscious relationship. These are not clearly defined or described like the separate parts of an engine, but rather intertwined in all we experience. They require discipline on our part and they will reflect where we are in our personal evolution of getting to know who we are. I'll try to explain them through insights.

Be willing to look at yourself and how you created what you currently experience in your relationship.

Notice a pattern of similar behaviours, without judging yourself or your partner, and ask yourself what the underlying spiritual lesson might be here for *you*.

Create internal feedback resources
Without violating the free will of your partner, allow yourself to be free from your need for approval or disagreement with your partner's opinion. These are useful frames that will bring us back to an empowered state, which will allow us to focus on the solution

rather than the obstacles. Write it down somewhere to remind yourself where the emotions come from.

Know that your partner can never hurt you. Everything you feel comes from your own experiences in the past and what you choose to believe about them. Choose to act in a kind and loving way towards your partner and take the time you need to heal inside using your own connection to God Source. Test whether you give your power away by noticing the degree to which you experience pain, and choose to take it back. Notice where you struggle to contain your emotions or wish to blame your partner and express to them that this reflection of you needs healing. The more you can own your projections as you express, the more love your partner can experience with you as you transform in front of them. Don't be afraid to take time out for self-reflection, to enable yourself to grow.

The more responsible you become, the more you will take your power back and become truly free in your relationship.

Accept your shadow

Notice how urges, reactions, thoughts, impulses, feelings and perceptions of our rejected self show up as the shadow. Practise the discipline of observing yourself, and consciously redirect the shadow that surfaces now, as you are ready to heal it with love and acceptance. To master the conscious mind allows it to know our true power and identity.

Notice when you don't feel like you're enough, that it's time to connect inside in order to nurture self-love. Recognise this as need, not love.

We don't enter our relationships to sap energy from one another, but rather as givers of energy to share together. We nurture ourselves by strengthening our relationship to Source. Remember, no matter how much your partner loves you, this lack of knowing yourself can only be satisfied with your connection to Source and not external love from someone else. External love is a reflection of your connection with yourself.

Live with spiritual integrity
No matter what the situation is, nothing is an excuse to act outside of the integrity you've defined for yourself. Do we tell our partners what they want to hear to gain their approval and support, or do we tell them the truth? Your words should be a true reflection of your personal needs and feelings.

We measure against ourselves and conduct ourselves in alignment to the best of our knowledge, in a way that doesn't violate any free will rights of others for our own interest.

Trust life to teach you freedom
Give up all entitlement rights to any promises made by your partner, including expectations or what you think they owe you. Know that in any given moment you have everything you need in abundance, so don't force your expectations of life onto your partner. Instead, notice even the smallest gifts from your partner and appreciate them. Give what you can from abundance to open the energy channels in the relationship, and you will receive the same energy, only amplified. Find ways to see the joy in what you have with your partner.

Freedom allows a new game of co-creation
Learn to co-create in divine right time without demanding, being patient. If it doesn't come now, then there's a reason for that.

Kindness is the gift we first give to ourselves and then to our partners. Always hold a vision of beauty even when it looks like there is no hope. This electrical high frequency creates a backflow of more loving kindness that maintains our freedom.

Everything, good and bad, is an expression of Source energy. It all deserves to be respected equally, no matter which level of awareness it has reached. Appreciate your body and that of your partner and what goes into them.

Cultivate tolerance for your partner to co-create with you equally, to fulfil her needs and desires.

Express with your partner, in all aspects of your life, as you learn to differentiate between your truth and the illusion of reality.

Maintaining freedom in your relationship is of the utmost importance and mastering what it takes to keep from falling back into a self-serving situation that will drain our power and energy, is a big part of knowing who we can be and what our relationships can become.

Conclusion

- Keep identities individual, honouring unique needs.
- Understand the magic of the mutual purpose in the relationship.
- Make yourself happy.
- Expect nothing from your partner.
- Appreciate and celebrate what your partner contributes.
- Test boundaries against their original intention.
- Respect each other's boundaries even when you don't understand them.
- Accept your partner as she is.
- Listen empathetically to your partner without offering unsolicited advice, and hold the potential for her to reach her own solutions.
- Witness your partner's growth with compassion.

- Don't take any expressions personally. Look inside for your own projections and pull them back, if possible.
- Give your partner the freedom to express herself as her free will guides her.
- Know that deep down you and your partner want the same thing.
- See your partner as an extension of yourself.
- Realise that what triggers you in your partner's behaviour is for your own personal development.
- Connect with your core regularly.
- Speak what you know to be the truth.
- Be gentle and kind with what you share, and be patient.
- Don't hold your partner accountable for her promises.
- Give from abundance and never what you need to sustain yourself. Then it is better not to give.
- Hold a vision of beauty when things appear to get ugly.

Chapter 14

I open to the Creator

Despite my fears

Fears of rejection

And fears of feeling my lack of love

But open I choose to stay

Beyond my unrealistic attachment to pain

So that it too can transmute into love

For nothing can resist the invitation

– Open Flower

Free Love

Intimacy creates the deepest level of connection two individuals can have when they both have equal power in a relationship built on love. Sex, love and compassion, the levels of appreciation in intimate connection, can all express the unique dynamics of developing intimacy in an open, honest, conscious relationship.

It is a dance between masculine and feminine that evolves through many levels with no one excluding the other as they move up the ladder of evolution.

Two people connect intimately to invite a higher presence
My personal experience of connecting started with my ability to connect with God Source. The more I opened and learned to trust life to teach me, and opened my heart to express my feelings to the world, I discovered that connecting can go all the way until we feel one with all that literally exists around us. We realise that nothing in this world is truly separate from anything else and that even relationships and the way we connect are still only in their infancy. People love to meditate because of how it makes them feel. Men love to make love because expressing themselves in this domain gives them another way of saying how much they love their

partners. Some men focus so much on themselves and releasing themselves that I wonder what they will make of my words. For a brief few seconds your mind is filled with pleasure hormones and you live from one high to the next. When separated from its deeper spiritual meaning, sex is always just sex. Love can be experienced when we give to our partner for their sake, rather than just *plug in*. When we love our partners and wish to support them, by expressing ourselves without masks, and they love us back for who we are, it is a **mutually satisfying experience** for both parties. When you make love with a partner who can feel what you feel and *hear* your thoughts in these moments of nakedness, and still look at you with love that enables you to express yourself any way you please, it is an even deeper reflection from which to experience your deepest passion.

Making love can be an expression of intimacy

Because making love is not mechanical to me, meaning it is not something I do, I have never had the same sexual experience twice. I look at my partner and see all that I can without intimidating him. I smell as much as I can and I listen to every time he breathes shallow or deep, faster or slower. I feel the rhythm of his movements and melt under his touch. I respond to his body, his words and his intentions. I notice when he shaves or doesn't shave or when he has a haircut. I let him feel appreciated.

In fact, I say and do all I would for me to me. I am gentle most of all and sometimes I want him not to hold back at all and see if he can match my softness with his focus and directive approach. If I want to take the lead, I let him know by increasing the movements of my hips so that he can follow my lead, and be soft when I am hard.

Making love requires as much mental presence and listening as any other form of communication we engage in. My partner and I probably learn more about the types of conversations we can have from our flawless love-making sessions than we can from teachers or books.

The beautiful thing about the body is that it cannot lie. Body wisdom has its own agenda and readiness for growth. We should never expect one another to perform a service, but instead take responsibility for our own neediness.

Osho said that one should have a room dedicated to making love. It sounds grand because it would probably be an environment free from the baggage or triggers that distract us from the purpose of the room. If you can dedicate a room maybe you can dedicate time too. Sometimes things cannot be rushed and at other times the anticipation leaves little room to play.

What is important is the appreciation of the moments as they present themselves, whether on the couch or the kitchen table. Everyone has their own preference. What I have come to value is the joy of sharing thoughts and fantasies as much as the act itself. My partner shares some of his thoughts, previously not said out loud, and I indulge him. I know that thoughts can create as much as actions can. I wish to share all of me with all of my partner. Any hidden thoughts are in the field between us anyway and can create resistance. By inviting him to share his fantasies with me, it allows me to experience a bit more of him, and accepts more of me to love indirectly.

Respect for each other allows us to connect freely
The most important thing to remember when we are open and vulnerable to each other is always to be respectful and treat someone else and their body as we would our own. It's easy to feel good about ourselves if we can put someone else down, but this comes from separation and competition. What I'm talking about is staying open even when what our partner reflects hurts us. We heal in these magic moments if we choose openness when we feel like closing. These open moments of growth liberate us and keep us free when we connect intimately. Anything is possible between

two people when we come from love. There are no limits to what we can experience when love is *made*, respectfully.

Our minds are powerful at creating events for us in which to play and experience each other fully and physically. There are few things that are as easy, that allow us to feel as alive and human, and assist our bonding experience with each other.

A woman will bring a man to his spirit-body and a man will bring a woman back into her earth-body when she is irrational.

A woman who feels beautiful has certain magic about the way she carries herself that has little to do with her appearance. What a woman feels inside, combined with her capacity to connect intimately with a man, is also called sex appeal.

A vulnerable woman can be really powerful when she is true to her nature as a person and radiates a soft openness that invites masculine penetration to open her even more.

The accountability to be physically intimate

I could never understand why men would enter any woman who made herself available, although I have met men whom, I think, might not engage with them. The choice to take up an offer or not comes from the spiritual integrity each person holds himself accountable to.

As a woman I have been in many situations where the only person to know my actions was me, and I didn't succumb to the apparent temptation because I held onto my self-respect.

I have also learned that there is something special about a woman who doesn't give herself to just any man who desires her. I'm not speaking about a game of resistance to attain a man. A virtuous woman is desirable by all men, even those who have no morals. But she is also the choice of those who have high standards.

According to David Deida, women who *save themselves* have a pure frequency. He even goes so far as to say that she can dissipate her energy by hugging other men. Some say it's a smell and hormonal in nature. I don't know the physical and chemical reasons; I only know that when a woman enters a room with this kind of pure frequency it is as if men can sense her purity. There is no judgement here; I only wish to address the fact that our choices have implications and the impact of openness with men without clear boundaries about the quality of our engagements has an emotional, physical, intellectual and spiritual nature. Women crave intimacy and it affects the frequency they radiate, which in turn makes them more, or less, desirable to the opposite sex.

The power to connect intimately comes from pure essence
Frequent love making with her partner cuts her off from other men mentally, emotionally and physically. She filters them out and lives for her partner. If she neglects her connection with Source, her innocence is compromised and her partner starts to notice other women.

When I was young, the neighbour's wife told me to dress well for my husband. I think in her mind she thought that this was the reason her husband had affairs while she raised six children. Men cheat because they start to feel unfulfilled by their women. Nothing is ever that simple, and there is no excuse for cheating. Each woman has her own needs. The skills she lacks to express them are perceived as nagging or whining, which drains her innocence and radiance. Any selective hearing on your part should be an indication that your women cannot express her needs clearly.

The desire to connect intimately for women
Intimacy is a woman's deepest desire and there are many love languages, of which touch is one. I can hear you saying that it's the

same for men. Indeed, it's as my partners have taught me. A man also desires a woman's touch to connect with her deeply and intimately, but at other times he may wish to be a man about town, or a wildling as I call it ... this is true for some more than others. I read recently that freedom is doing what we like. However, happiness is loving what we do. Life is filled with choices. Once we have lived, we know what exercising our options feels like, and when we decide we are conscious about the consequences of our actions, we choose wisely.

To connect intimately, and not get lost in the unknown, we need to know who we are on an even deeper level. When a man connects with a woman he connects through her to something deeper. He connects to whatever frequency she connects to. Together, in their union, they tap into a Source energy, which he cannot draw on his own this powerfully. It is a very intimate experience for which women open themselves wide.

Nothing gives her more pleasure than to receive what a man has to give in the presence of truth, and to let all that she is flow back to him.

Every physical connection you make with other people keeps you connected energetically until you break it consciously on every level. When a woman gives a man permission to enter her, it will always leave her vulnerable to this man, so she needs to be able to trust him. It is her responsibility to use her power wisely. Her power will be to choose who she opens herself to and who she does not open to, to keep her frequency pure. How a man responds to it later to his friends can impact on her in many ways and will reflect whether he treats her with respect. Sometimes getting a woman to open is only the start. Getting her to open again and again, to penetrate her with your love, requires more skill and authenticity and trust.

Often after disagreements, when we've kissed and made up, I am reminded that no matter how cold I experience my partner to be, or how cold he told me I was; we needed the same thing. We needed love. We need to be held in a way that we feel completely accepted for who we are, and not to be changed in any way. Although we might not have to hear we are special, except from our partners because they chose us, we feel perfect in every way. Love will affect everyone, even when people try to keep a poker face. There is no power like softness to break down the walls of the heart.

Our nature is to be free to love

At this stage we accept that the nature of a man and a woman is what it is and that freedom in the relationship means she has to accept his nature and he chooses to accept her nature. What does that mean in terms of the father who saw his daughter's friend as beautiful? What does it give permission for and how does this relate to freedom?

David Deida, who wrote *The Way of the Superior Man*, says that men naturally desire sexual variety and should accept this as part of their nature. However, when in an intimate relationship with someone he loves, he needs to remember that the consequences of acting on those desires are seldom worth it.

A counter-argument comes from a study of children at Stanford University where four-year-olds were lead into a room one by one. They were offered two marshmallows if they waited for the person to return from an errand or one marshmallow right away. Later investigations, when those children were graduating from high school, when comparing those who waited with those who grabbed a marshmallow right away, proved that that those who had no impulse control had 210 (out of 1600) points lower on average compared to those who waited for two marshmallows. Later research showed that into their twenties, the kids with impulse control had better developed relationships, were more dependable and responsible, and showed better self-control in the face of frustration. The cost of impulsivity and distractedness interferes with our ability as a human species to learn and adapt.

This clearly indicates there is a difference between the immediate seeking of pleasure, or avoidance of pain, and using pre-frontal cortex thinking to determine the long-term impact of decisions.

There is of course no judgement on the person who wishes to pursue every woman his heart desires. What story he tells himself about the need behind it must hold up when it comes to his true nature to be deeply intimate with a partner. A partner's decision to act on an impulse will depend on the level of consciousness he has achieved.

For a female the freedom in a relationship relates to her willingness to open for a male partner of her choice when she is approached. Depending on her level of consciousness, she might make herself available to any willing partner who propositions her, or partners who are emotionally available to her or when the partner is fully mentally and emotionally present for her.

Personally, I respond to partners when I can experience all of that person with me; I am that kind of woman. Maybe for other women this is not necessary, but when I give all of me I hope to give it equally to a partner who will give all of him when he is with me. And maybe this is what *hard to get* women need who do not respond to most men's propositions. Maybe the ultimate woman needs the ultimate man – a man who can engage on all levels and stand before her in a way that she cannot see anything else. The right kind of connection is a match of frequency intensity. Just like a man can sense a woman's frequency, a woman can sense when a man's focus is entirely on her.

A woman senses if a man's focus is entirely on her, but how long can he hold a gaze before being distracted and will he match her intensity?

She feels if he can contain her energetically or if she still has energy left that can flow over and radiate in other directions.

For a man, the ultimate freedom would be to choose to be with various partners or not, to be completely in control of his chosen outcome for his experience with women. For a woman, complete freedom is to be completely vulnerable with the man of her choice. Or is it? Freedom is expressed in our connection through sexuality.

Sexual essence is promoted by the male when he praises and appreciates his partner's radiance, and by the female when she inspires and supports her partner. The contrary is also true according to David Deida, in his book *Intimate Communion*, when the male remarks that she looks drab or ugly. A woman, in turn, will emasculate her man when she doesn't trust his direction and questions him on it. It is human nature to experience depolarisation of the sexes, as humans adapt to their circumstances all the time. What was experienced in the mind, as a peak experience that laid new neurological patterns, now becomes ordinary. It makes sense to put effort into keeping our experiences of each other new and inviting to improve intimacy. She is more sensitive to your tone of voice than to your words. Notice when her mood shifts in response to your tone and use laughter to break down walls. Intimacy is ultimately more frequent, and deeper; it is embodied in experiences of each other to know each other right to the depths of our souls. Her ultimate desire is to be filled with love and that is what you embody when you open her.

Opening a woman for sexual intimacy

For a woman to open her heart space, she needs a man who can match her sexual essence. If you think that it's someone who loves you, think again, because in reality another person only reflects how much you love yourself. Opening a woman's heart allows her to experience love flowing out of her own heart. If she closes because of her own pain, it means that the love feeling goes away again and she will yearn for it. Our hearts are naturally open.

When a woman is radiant, she has already surrendered to love and opened her heart. Nothing else, no personal or work achievement, takes away the feelings of emptiness and aloneness like love does. More than anything else she desires to be overwhelmed by love, and even more so the more feminine her essence is. Making love, where she is matched by her intimate partner, is the ultimate full expression she can give to the love she is, when she opens her heart and expresses uninhibitedly with her body. What this means is that her partner also lets go of control and self-yielding to allow the ego to die and experience his own flowing love to the point where they merge in heart and soul. Some people say that when we make love we die, maybe this is why.

To give love is the most natural thing, but our experiences close us to the most magical intimate experience there is. To keep our hearts open, we connect to the highest part of ourselves, our internal connection to Source. When we do, love is infinite. To be truly satisfied and fulfilled we must each accept all of our parts, our darkest fears, aggressive natures and passions. Nothing must be suppressed because the one place suppressed feelings will show up is in the bedroom. Use this energy to channel into the love you surrender, to increase the intensity of intimacy you experience being naked emotionally, psychologically and spiritually in front of each other, to be complete mirrors for each other. This will liberate you from your own expectations of needing to know where you stand in your relationship to just be in the moment, fully present in love. This is the gift of intimacy.

Believe it or not, giving our gift of love is our responsibility.

The masculine gift to the feminine

The masculine gift is to penetrate the female heart. You can do this especially when she is closed and this allows her to give her love to you and to the entire world. Women are indecisive; their gifts are dancing in the moment. Men are the decision-makers who choose the path they take together. This is the purpose of the different types of energy. Did you know your main gift in intimacy is to guide your woman? She can help you get into your body and out of your mind when she lures you into her web, which will connect you to your deepest truth and Source. This will give you the depth and vision you need to fulfil your purpose. If you get lost in your thoughts and your world of work for too long, your work will lack substance. Don't try to pull away from her in your head, but learn to stay present with her in her heart every moment as she gifts you. Truly live with abandon. But don't forget to go to your man cave and be with men, as this will enhance your masculine nature and keep you polarised. She will trust you as you guide her to play with her girlfriends, to keep her feminine essence alive and vibrant.

Concluding boundaries of free love

How do you score when it comes to boundaries?
1. Do you have bedroom etiquette? What are the habits you keep?
2. Are you fully present making love, in mind, body and heart?
3. Do you gift your partner without thinking of your own impulses?
4. Are you aware of another dimension when you connect intimately with your partner that makes you feel alive?
5. Are you free to express yourself in your love-making?
6. Does your partner feel free to express her needs during love-making?
7. Do you explore and discover more of yourself during love-making?
8. Do you trust your partner with your fantasies?
9. Do you give up easily or role-play to discover new ways to open your partner?
10. How do you respond when your partner whines?
11. What do you do to contribute to your partner's radiance? Do you still notice it? Do you appreciate it verbally?

12. Can you sense a pure woman when she passes you? Do you desire to be intimate with her? How do you respond?
13. Do you understand how to be intimate with women by understanding clear boundaries?
14. Do you match the intensity of your partner's desire to be intimate with her? What informs your answer? When last did you ask her?
15. Can you stay present to stare without being distracted?
16. Do you experience fulfilment in your lovemaking?
17. Do you consciously make love to gift your woman by opening her when she is closed?
18. Do you become more intimate each time you make love?

PART THREE

Understanding What Is

Behind Her Triggers

Chapter 15

How do we get there...?

The secret is that you are never not there

It is always with and inside you

You just remember or find yourself having to ask for it

– What Is Heart Space

What Is This Constant Need for Appreciation?

Understanding women, or even one woman, is a virtuous goal indeed. Her depth really is like the ocean and all you will ever see are the waves on the surface. She will allow you to ride her and just as easily engulf you with her huge waves if you're not proficient enough to surf them, so pay attention to her innuendos.

Has she accepted her nature to nurture?
In principle a woman's soft nature invites you to expect nurturing and her body reflects this intrinsic nature in her external appearance. It naturally baffles the mind when she seems to be in constant need of appreciation. What is all that about? It shows up as subtle hints and a dark mood that you can't quite understand. Sometimes, no matter what a man tries to do, it just seems to go on and on. To her it feels like she is like an ATM machine where everyone comes to draw money. Everyone takes according to his or her own needs and no one ever comes to make a deposit.

Understanding her own needs through projection

Her inability to express her need is projected onto you for her to learn on the outside what she doesn't know about herself inside. She complains and you feel the urge to do what you do best: fix it. If she keeps complaining you develop selective hearing and a wall builds up between you. When this starts to happen there is something you can do, and this listening is easier and subtler than you can imagine. It will be an investment in the conscious currency of your relationship.

Finding her way to inner appreciation

When a woman hasn't yet learned to keep her heart open and experience herself as a flowing river of love, she craves attention and affection. When she is connected to her own inner source of nurturing, she will give whatever kind of nurturing is requested. When her nurturing skills haven't matured, receiving the appreciation that she so intensely desires allows her to feel beautiful. And it is this feeling of knowing her beauty that needs understanding. Unless she has discovered a way to keep her heart open, where she feels her own love reflected to her by others, she keeps searching for someone who can open her with the same intensity that she desires to keep the flow alive.

In today's society of stress stimulants and role confusion, each person has to find their own way to sustain and nourish his or her own needs. Our happiness is our own responsibility, as mentioned many times because it's so important. Women are at an advantage to support themselves better financially today, but they still do it according to the rules of directive and focussed performance that represents a masculine energy. This leaves her with little room to practise being a feminine, leading woman when being at work cultivates a masculine energy within her. In order to be open she needs to be in her feminine energy and, without a roadmap, the possibility of being a feminine leader might not even occur to her.

To recognise what is missing in her life she needs to choose to create an environment that will support her open heart.

How she learns about her beauty

It is men, not women, who will teach a woman about her beauty. A woman's first lesson in appreciation comes from her father when he appreciates her beauty: the first few turns she makes, and every time he comments on her dress and smiles. She will do anything to see herself through her daddy's eyes and falls in love with this image of herself. As an adult she transfers her female appreciation to her beau. Now the need for appreciation falls on his shoulders until the day comes that she can do it for herself. So there you have it gentlemen: now you know why you have so much power over your partner and it's up to you to use it wisely until the time comes for her to take it back.

Encourage her to take her power back

Most women never know that they can or should do this for themselves. They reach independence on so many levels and still don't learn to trust men to provide for them or nurture their emotional needs, because of past hurts from their perspective. True independence happens in their minds, and until they realise that they need to take their power back, something is always missing. I left for Peru in celebration of my 40th birthday. I wanted to go by myself and I guess in a way I wanted to take my self-respect back. For too long I had allowed a man to take care of me. I was no longer sure who I was or where and how I fitted in. I felt dissatisfied with my life. I had so much and still it was not enough. I spent hours in solitude trying to connect with something that would give me a sense of self. Doing something rather than thinking about it, I thought would show where the lack of alignment was between my thoughts and actions. So I set off for Peru as a novice traveller.

A lot went wrong. Even before I left the airport I realised my return trip times were overlapping in a bad way. After arriving in New York I discovered my hotel was misrepresented by the website. I was stuck inside a hotel room too ugly to cry in. Looking back, I have to laugh at the irony. I was a spoiled little brat with so little appreciation of what my life offered and I rejected so much that was reflected to me. First I found a more suitable hotel room, although it was still not what I was accustomed to, but at least it was within my budget. The room was white with an en-suite bathroom and had no flowers or paintings on the walls for some colour. But it felt safe. It took me three days to find the beauty inside myself to settle down, after many tears and much self-control to not swamp the room with fresh flowers. That was indeed a mini lesson of what was to come in my month away from home on my own.

At the beginning of my workshop in Peru with Gregg Braden, after inquiring why I was there, he advised me to seek an answer to the question "What will complete me?" I meditated on this with every opportunity of solitude, in very sacred places, as much as I could. I guess I was waiting for some inner light bulb moment that never came. It was only on my flight home and in later reflection that I felt my heart opening wide. I didn't find any solutions to my inner questions, but something other than what I expected was happening to me. I fell in love with myself again – so completely in love that I could see the beauty of it all. I realised that I had to go through letting go of any expectations of what I thought I might find. I needed to prepare myself to be completely pure on the inside in every way I understood. Only then did I discover inside me what I was looking for on the outside: I could see my own beauty. This was not the first time I had realised this, but at this time I was aware that it was my heart that opened again. At the time of my heart opening I really and truly felt fulfilled inside myself.

The need for appreciation is a soul desire
Something else that was magical happened to me on that 14-hour trip back to Johannesburg from New York: I wrote 15 poems. They were just flowing out of me. I wrote for no purpose but to express my bliss. I wrote until I fell asleep. I resisted sleeping because I didn't want to wake up not feeling this incredible love. When I came back to South Africa, my Facebook page attracted almost 5000 friends over the course of the next month as a result of sharing my thoughts and I started a fan page. I finally felt fulfilled and appreciated. When I experienced this rich, beautiful inner world, it didn't matter what was happening outside me, or who wanted what; I was happy and the world was a beautiful place.

Recognising her closed heart
I learned that my open heart was magnetic and during those times I experienced an appreciation of myself. When I notice that I need some attention or appreciation from my partner, I now know that I don't feel like I am quite enough. I built up resistance towards my partner, because it felt like I gave so much and it wasn't appreciated. During those times I recognised my closed heart. In working with women on these issues as a coach, I realised just how needy and energetically draining women can be. One day a young lady admitted to me that she came to my workshop because she wanted to see what energy she could get. The very same girl later stopped coming because she chose to go to another workshop where she felt she could get what she wanted. She loved my energy, but criticised me for (her words) my "Buddhist view" on life. She promised to pray for me. Since I consider myself more spiritual than religious I could only smile at the comments. I realised that many women still give their power away and exchange energy when it's attaching them to what they think will save them.

To receive appreciation one needs to be able to appreciate one's self first

As long as we believe that love is outside of us or that someone else can give it to us, we will risk being trapped by giving our power to someone else. To experience the ultimate form of appreciation we need to learn to do it for ourselves. Our partner can teach us what the feeling feels like, which gives us a mind map of their experience. To sustain the feeling, we need to create the flow from our heart and feel our own appreciation for ourselves. Enlightenment is one of my favourite reading topics and I read the story of the Buddha transformation in every book I can get my hands on. I realise that one of the most magical experiences through our physiological, neurological, chemical reactions and thought reflections is when the lights go on inside us. My various experiences have one thing in common – a feeling of being more special than I had ever been able to imagine I was, until now. When a power higher than our physical body, in any which way you choose to describe or define it, reflects how we are appreciated, our entire perspective about life changes in that moment. It is as if we are flooded with wonderful emotions and dopamine in a most overwhelming way, without short-circuiting our brain. Maybe one day science will find the exact recipe and recreate it for us. Ervin Laslo, who experimented with psychedelics and breathing techniques, has written some of the most significant interdisciplinary work on what is out there in books like *The Akashic Field*. It is as if the feeling of being appreciated is almost a requirement to experience these extraordinary moments of connection to something bigger than our physical bodies.

A map for appreciation

The first time I was overcome with the incredible feeling that I was worth more than I thought I was, I had a hypnotherapy session with a psychologist. All that had happened to me, and all that I believed, was forgiven and overridden with love in a few hours as my heart opened. In that very same session I had a vision of a moment in my future, which I experienced five years later. Ervin Laslo describes this kind of out-of-body experience as the *Akashic fields*, and other people use different words. I searched for two years after I had this experience to understand what I saw, until I was directed to Ervin Laslo's work. These brave men are prepared to share their innermost experiences for everyone to have a map of what is possible. The idea that appreciation might be the DMT (Dimethytryptamine) hormone for the brain like endorphins are for the body when we exercise, proposes that we do an exercise to experience it for ourselves instead of expecting it from our partners. Maybe as a male you already know this, but it can also guide your woman to experience her sense of self. People have different ways of feeling deeply alive and when they integrate it into their lives, it shifts their perspective and appreciation of self. It is the lack of this sense of fulfilment of soul and meaning that gives rise to the side effects that result from addictive behaviours, depression and allowing ourselves to be abused. Whichever way this roadmap shows up, it is how we make sense of it and receive the appreciation that frees us from expecting it from our partner. When you offer it to your partner she can receive your gift with the pure intention you offered it.

How to appreciate the ultimate woman

I was asked in an interview what a man gives a radiant beautiful woman who has everything. For a few moments I was observing the fear of a man who was not sure of himself. I told him that the image that comes up for me is Catherine Zeta-Jones receiving a necklace or flowers from her lover. Why that came up was because when a woman radiates, her satisfaction of life radiates off her and she appears to need nothing. A woman like that can make any man feel right at home and at ease as she appreciates even the smallest token he offers and what she really receives is the heart with which he gives it. The purity she senses is equal to her own and she has the wisdom to recognise that. Can you buy that with money? She might prefer the time you took to stop and handpick flowers for her or make her laugh. A man who does that will mirror her soul and she will open even more.

Keep a space for faith
When you think your partner isn't there yet, hold space in your heart for her to discover and appreciate herself; it will happen in her own time.

Every time you offer to help her instead of just listening, you create something else for her to focus on or blame. Appreciating her here might just mean that you don't offer any information, which will turn her inwards to reflect. Hope needs to exist visibly for that one moment when the person who needs to break through can lift her out of her illusion in an act of grace. The moment your partner experiences your appreciation will be when she realises what you were hoping she would understand. Yes, she's a beautiful paradox. Don't allow her to be dependent on you for her appreciation-fix, but guide her to keep her heart open and experience the flow of constant appreciation for herself. Know also that she will appreciate you in those moments even more because she will recognise in you what you reflect to her, more than she has noticed it before, as appreciation in its deepest and most fulfilling way. Where possible, allow her to keep it open. Be mindful of the stresses of daily life and maintain the balance necessary to stay open yourself.

She focusses first on relationships
Women don't shift between their purpose and their relationship. You are her biggest purpose. Her work is something she does for her family.

Appreciate her for her loving ways and presence in the moment. Allow her to indulge in flowers and objects of beauty and a different sense of time. Appreciate all the little things that are noticed by no one else, and even allow her whining to be the red flags that tell you it will take a special appreciation to help her open her heart again.

Find your partner's love language and learn to show her you love her with your time, gifts or comments about how she looks. Suggest she does something for herself because she deserves to nurture herself.

Conclusion

- Understanding a woman is a virtuous goal.
- Her apparent irrational behaviour comes from not accepting the responsibility to nurture herself.
- Through her projection she expects you to give her what she needs, instead of expressing it directly.
- By ignoring her she might never learn to ask outright for what she needs or never discover that she can give this to herself.
- Her need for appreciation is a soul craving.
- Until she learns how to open her own heart, she will be dependent on you to give her this appreciation.
- When she pulls her projection back she will open her heart by herself.
- Her craving for intimate appreciation will never stop – it drives her behaviour.
- She blames you when she cannot see her own reflection. If you defend yourself, it will become worse.
- If you don't lead her, she will develop her own masculine to lead her.
- There is nothing you can do to fulfil her need for appreciation for long, but be her willing life partner to be projected onto so she can come to her own realisations. Don't take her comments personally but stay present.
- You can teach her about her beauty. She sees herself through your eyes. This will assist her to appreciate herself. Allow her

to tell you about her map of herself and, as she does, she will discover more about herself. Encourage her self-expression.
- When women learn to nurture themselves, they become good nurturers to their families.
- Mirror her soul.
- Keep penetrating her with the intention to open her heart.
- If she even glimpses that you have succeeded, she will test you to see if you can sustain it.
- Believe in her. Know that your relationship always comes first for her. Everything she does is for your relationship, even when it hides behind work agendas.
- Pick her flowers – don't buy them.

Chapter 16

Learn from the silence

At peace with the all that is

Time has no significance

Become one with sounds of creation

Colours of love everywhere

Even the blind can see

I cannot perceive it

I see only my needs in your shadow

– What Would Happen if I Screamed

What Does It Mean When She Says That She Doesn't Feel Seen And Heard?

Daddy's little girl needs attention. Until she matures she will need you to help her heal her issues as she experiences what they felt like again.

There are different ways that we connect with our partners. Some couples realise that they have values in common. Others match their feminine receptive energy with the masculine directive and focussed gaze, and the dance begins.

Love is the movement that evolves us to grow as individuals. If you notice and hear her for just the right amount of time without intimidating her, she can receive your love. That initial in-love stage is there for a very long time after you've conquered her, and she is yours.

Each time her heart closes, it needs to be heard and seen in the same way for it to open again to receive your love. Of course, this is not always your priority as you focus on your purpose. This is, after all, why you need her as a diversion. But then she wants more…

Take time out rather than pretend to listen

"I don't feel heard and seen," she says, and you pretend to listen. You are there in body but not in mind and she isn't fooled; no half-hearted effort will do. You really do need to notice her, just like you do your little daughter, until she grows out of it. If you cannot do it being fully mentally present, excuse yourself and allow her to struggle inside herself. It's her nature to want you to dance with her until you completely lose yourself in the moment. Then and only then will she let you go to fulfil your purpose. Even Rumi, the mystic poet said of his feminine essence, "There are lovers content with longing. I am not one of them." Now it isn't your language of love she needs but to fill the longing of her soul.

She cannot feel heard or seen until she understands the underlying lesson of her spirit.

She doesn't know how to articulate this need to you in words, as it's an underlying longing feeling. In her heart she knows there is something that she needs to see and hear. You're the closest mirror that reflects her actions. Inside she's feeling empty without it. Her intuition is leading her on to notice where and how she is to act in this moment. If she looks at the reflection of her appointed clearest mirror (you), it may be a guide to her own deepest insights.

The inability to hear comes from the pain of shutting down

Our need to be heard and seen comes from places in our past that hurt us. My biological father died when I was two years old. From my earliest memories I remember singing in church, hardly able to see over the first row of seats, with my sister. We sang an Afrikaans song that translates into "Jesus, make me a sunray to shine". I remember how quiet it became as people heard our voices and I remember specifically how I felt having so many eyes fixed on me. It was probably my first real taste what it is like to have people's full attention focussed on me.

My mother had her hands full with three children and there was never much time for individual bonding. I have no doubt that this experience was the equivalent of what other little girls experience when their daddies swing them in the air, noticing how adorable they are.

Your partner's need to be heard and seen by you is only reflecting her deep need to acknowledge herself. The need to express can be very strong if a child is constantly told to be seen and not heard, or to suppress her feelings. What I'm aware of is how much this experience drove my need to be heard and seen in life, including how often I shied away from being seen. It talks to our core human need to have a sense of belonging just because we are, and not because we do something.

Fears are empty when we look at them directly
Our minds will be at ease when we truly understand our pain, but understand that pain is an emotion in our energy field and needs a reason to exist. We'll always ask why something bad happened or try to be understood for our own behaviour.

I love the St Francis Prayer where it says, "God, let me understand rather than be understood." It allows me to let go of pain to open my heart again in moments when it is difficult. Our past comes up for healing when we're ready for it.

I believe our need to be seen and heard as women is deeply linked to healing moments of old wounds about the masculine to accept more of who we are. Healing doesn't mean that we forgive and forget as a doing experience, but rather being with what is.

If you allow your partner time to express what she feels, she might experience the pain that creates the emptiness inside her. Expressing our old beliefs about why we think the hurt occurred in the first place is not as important as questioning the meaning we made from what happened to us.

We try to live with what happened, because it's what made sense to us at the time. But the pain is still there, which means that we jumped to a conclusion that might no longer serve us. There is nothing to stop us making a more useful meaning from an informed place if we're willing to revisit that old pain by 'un-storying' it as adults.

Witnessing with love heals

Real healing can be witnessed when we can find a way to hold ourselves, and the injured parts of the world, in our hearts. Keeping our hearts open when it hurts is what allows us to see and hear ourselves. Healing teaches us to live fully, through sharing with our partner intimately, from the ability *to be*, no matter how hard it seems to us.

The truth is that we don't always know why bad things happen, but we can make them count. By making them count we can see and hear ourselves as women. What we really do when we open our heart is open to life again and get our mojo and radiance back.

What we try so hard to avoid is where we find the answers we seek

We pass through emptiness en route to opening our hearts. It is this emptiness we try to avoid, or fill, at all costs by doing stuff like drugs, drama or alcohol. It's also in this emptiness that we desire to see and hear ourselves. Falling through it is easier than it sounds. After my first husband died, I didn't sleep for 21 days. I was terrified of going to sleep, forgetting he would not be there in the morning. I didn't want to wake up to find that he was lost to me again. It was as if I could still feel his presence and I just didn't want to let go. So I went out and stayed out all night long. I filled my time with doing stuff and created a lot of drama for myself. I just couldn't deal with what I didn't know and would find any work that needed to be done to keep my mind from going there.

What was it I feared exactly? What was it that I saw and heard in the despair and grief that overwhelmed me? The questions I could not answer touched the immortality of my soul. It was in this very centre of the vast emptiness that I found a still sanctuary that reminded me of who I really was.

Each person has to find their own special way to get to their centre. For me it was Peru and Hawaii on my vision quests. Now it is as simple as spending time alone connecting with myself and my fears. Some meditate and some pray. I used to think I meditated until I realised that focussed stillness is mediation and prayer is a more open listening. Whatever we choose to practise, we need to commit to regular, structured activity, even when we don't feel like it. Perseverance without expectation will allow seeing and hearing ourselves at the same time that we are present with our inner resistance. Entering the emptiness requires that we let go.

Let's just define stillness: it doesn't mean that we do something. Meditation is not about lighting a candle and folding your legs – it's about allowing thoughts without trying to control them, just observing them. Or we can fill the stillness with too much doing and then we are back where we originally ask our partners to see and hear us because we're unable to. The point of stillness is to hear and see ourselves. Then we will feel heard and seen by everyone around us. How can we ask our partners to do for us what we cannot do for ourselves?

> ∽*If we can simply be with the fear that we are not enough, and with the vastness of what we do not know, we discover an emptiness that is not failure but is the very source of the fullness of who and what we are.*
> *– "The Dance" by Oriah Mountain Dreamer* ∽.

You may not be able to save her – only she can save herself
Really opening our hearts means that we are willing to open them to ourselves and accept each situation for what it is. Inner strength for women comes from choosing to be at peace with what we have and, at the same time, to choosing life itself. Always recognise her whining as a sign that she is ready to heal herself and you are her witness.

Summary
You give her attention, but she wants more. If you cannot witness her being fully present in that moment, excuse yourself and allow her to struggle by herself. It is her nature to ask you, her appointed life-mirror, to give her the presence her soul longs for to fill the emptiness she feels. Remember that at this point she is unable to give it to herself. She needs to learn the underlying soul lesson by entering the emptiness and feeling the pain that results from not recognising her own love. As partner, you are her appointed teacher in this regard. She wants her masculine to accept more of her, the parts she rejected that pain her, with his witnessing gaze. She needs to make the pain count by seeing and hearing herself as a woman as she opens her heart again to tell a new, empowering story. She can no longer avoid what touches the immortality of her soul and she will find the sanctuary inside her of who she really is, eventually. Time alone will grant her the experience to face her own fears and hear herself. She can do this by committing to a structure that allows her to listen *inwards* and be present with her inner resistance to being alone and letting go of what she tries to control. She will learn that she cannot ask her partner to do what she cannot do for herself. This is one of the wonderful benefits of having a partner. As you witness with her, one plus one becomes more than two. Even as adults, in a relationship, we still have the privilege of expressing as children, to heal and to have each other's backs.

Of course, telling her this might mean little. But if you can understand it, it makes all the difference in the world to have empathy for her struggle with her own soul. Living what we understand is more valuable than knowing it.

Chapter 17

A dragonfly sitting behind an elephant's ear

A team invincible

Elephant step into lightness

A dragonfly is not a butterfly

To name the untouchable

Sense innocence pure

Just the other side

Of the door in my heart

It is my way out

This inward way

Free from borders

Revealing vulnerability

Beauty has no bounty

Courage is free

Humility is my key

Awareness the only currency

– Fly Dragon Fly

Fly Dragon Fly –
Her Dragonfly Transformation

Humans have long learned through symbols and nature. In fact, urban shamans and Buddhas in bikinis read all sorts of messages metaphysically in nature. For me, the start of the female voice inside became more visible through figuring out the message of the dragonfly in nature. And just as the dragonfly has a specific vibration, the feminine voice also has a specific energy signature.

Stages of transformation

I discovered that dragonflies are special creatures that live for a very short time. Some species start off as eggs then turn into larvae for about four years, which then turn inside out to become little illuminated insects.

These insects live for about two months. It seems to be an awfully long preparation period for a short adult life cycle. But they are the fastest flying and most precise flying insects in the insect world.

According to legend dragonflies take and bring messages to and from the gods.

Symbolic meaning of the dragonfly

For me the transformation of the dragonfly is not like that of the butterfly. Where the butterfly seems to be carefree, the dragonfly is purposeful. To have the kind of transformation that turns you inside out seems like the feminine that opens her heart willing to feel her emptiness, which is then filled with love that flows until it closes again. These strange little creatures were attracted to me at each of my milestones, which made me wonder more about them. All I know for sure is that the dragonflies showed up as I started my inward journey to find myself, which earmarked what became a journey of learning to open my heart and keep it open. The dragonfly transformation became my symbol for female transformation.

The four wings of the dragonfly symbolise the four elements that keep transformed women flying. They can be presented as:

- Learning the skills of how to nurture herself, as taught by motherhood
- How to reflect consciously in relationships to learn who she really is
- Developing her natural feminine leadership style (in contrast to the commonly accepted masculine way of leading in business)
- Experiencing herself as intimate by living passionately and sensually in spiritual daily practice.

The next segment of the body represents the bridging of the transformation that prepares women for emotional freedom. The focus is on the inner process and struggles to create the gateway to the next step of expression. Just like the dragonfly is larva for four years, this process has its own time frame.

I also realised that women were not yet ready to experience this change inside themselves. Your partner needs a new mental map of how she could be different, first to bridge any big decisions, before she will be brave enough to transform herself.

With more gender equality in the workplace this need to transform can be identified at a different level to bridge the poverty consciousness so many woman experience inside themselves, before they are ready to start nurturing themselves. But the deep work is the same – getting a woman to understand her own needs and learning how to meet them. And that is exactly where relationships can play a significant role in getting women to become more conscious.

Your co-creative relationship can develop new and conscious roles unlike any you were taught by your parents. By practising with the purest of intentions, you will both find yourselves on an adventure that will change your lives forever.

I've already mentioned that the female has physical triggers that activate the transformation to coincide with psychological development. These stages that progress, one at a time, take place with an underlying spiritual lesson.

Women have no choice but to engage with their inner struggle until they understand the moral lesson that I will refer to as a rite of passage, embedded deep in the subconscious mind.

The logical brain applies intuitive understanding from the creative part of the brain, as each rite of passage is integrated. But at no stage is she ready to take the journey, until no other choice remains. This is the part of development where there is knowledge but it's not yet embodied, or where in Anais Nin's terms the pain to stay closed in a bud is more painful than the pain needed to open the flower.

The philosophical perspective of inner masculine and feminine

The soul journey, of what I think of as the emerging feminine in the unconscious field, is just like the symbolic messages of the dragonflies that appeared and interacted with me. The transforming woman is learning the moral lessons of the inner world of the female struggle.

This is a story that describes the recovery of lost femininity in all women (or men) as they experience the triggers in life that call them inward.

Allow me to explain that feminine as referred to here, is the internal feminine side all men and women have, not just women. But more often than not, the story starts with her because she is more sensitive to hearing her soul's voice. As she develops on her journey, you too will be invited to join her in the symbolic meaning of the marriage of the bride and groom.

The biological triggers in the female body

As if the simultaneous journey of the spiritual and scientific perspectives doesn't give enough information for the feminine story, there is one bigger player that will start the inner journey. Triggers activate the journey. Sometimes this happens straight away and sometimes the journey goes inwards only years later. Her biology also shapes the feminine. The physical stages of life that set the stage for the inner story to take place for growth have a chronological life cycle, and at each intervention, all the baggage from the experience before is loaded onto what is coming up next.

These trigger events are:
- Birth
- Adolescence: physical female features and first menses
- First sexual experience
- Committing to a lifelong partner
- Birthing a child
- Menopause
- Death

Each stage is surrounded by intellectual and emotional growth in personality in order to adapt to the environment. For example, menopause is pre-empted by three years of emotional, irrational behaviour because of hormonal imbalances before the actual production of eggs stops. On a philosophical level, this is the Crone stage where the shadow side is represented by the part that has not yet matured, and wisdom is expressed through the healthy and grown side of the personality. Psychologically, if the person is not ready for this development, we refer to it as empty nest syndrome. My own inner journey was ignored when my first husband died. I was living it up with alcohol and late nights with friends just to not be alone with my thoughts. I didn't choose this journey, even though my circumstances triggered it by spending hours reflecting in hospitals. It's very much a voluntary choice to go inwards; no event or trigger can let us become conscious of going down the rabbit hole to find out how deep it is. The only thing that we can be certain of is that the opportunities in life will keep presenting themselves until the day we say yes. And if the last trigger is that of death and we have still not met our inner divine feminine, then I guess it wasn't meant to be in this lifetime. Some roads are just less travelled.

The emerging feminine
Always grateful to my ex-husband for his patience and honourable conduct, I still had to admit that our relationship was a mess. I

could never submit my masculine to his decisions, or accept his decisions with blind trust. I felt that if he couldn't value my input, I had to learn to step into taking responsibility for educating myself in matters that affected me. This was a new level of feminine that was strong and present in me, and testing the male archetype to trust my dignity and respect. In reality, my partner was only reflecting to me the inner struggle between my masculine and feminine. Typically, the roles played in the relationship were that of supportive feminine with a driving masculine. But my inner masculine was strong and because I was so conditioned to protect myself, it was difficult to submit to a man if he was not stronger than I was. What I had to learn was that as a woman my strength was in trusting my male, not fighting with him. This meant that I had to trust my own feminine to handle whatever may come. Now my ex-husband and I are better friends than ever, free to make decisions independently as my masculine was no longer competing with his.

In my drive to find myself, I discovered that no man can be God and I was in love with perfection and unrealistic expectations. I was infatuated with my image of the perfect integrated man, and if I couldn't have him, I'd rather have no one.

I had to learn to see beyond my projections to what was really there and learn to co-create with others. But for a woman to learn to trust a man, he has to be even stronger and more ruthless than her, and I was pretty strong by then. Or if I was to transform I had to trust my feminine to embrace whatever forceful, penetrating energy was coming my way as the emerging feminine inside me.

The emerging masculine

In the past, men would give me feedback that my spirit couldn't be contained. But when my new partner held onto me tightly one day in a frantic embrace, and said, "No matter how hard you push me away, I will never leave you," my fear of abandonment was staring back at me through his eyes. What I didn't know then was that I would learn to trust him and, in time, my own masculine, despite my circumstances to heal my own insecurities. I would learn that acceptance was the key to not being afraid and my heart was the measuring stick that would guide me when courage was not for action but wisdom.

The public persona of the developing feminine

The thing in the psyche of a woman that teaches us about following or not following, is what moves us through stages – from the virgin, to the mother, to the wise old woman. Maybe in society the ultimate icon or the innocent virgin was Mother Theresa or the mother Lady Diana. Notice that our society doesn't have a collective icon for the Crone or Medicine woman. The Crone collective is expressed as our shadow because it has been repressed and rejected by society and now we have to deal with her destructive female anger on a global level.

From here, young girls are informed by their mothers' shadow sides instead of constructive wisdom, which locks in the games women play, like withholding sex for favours.

The evolving woman starts off as the victim until she learns not to be afraid. She must find the courage inside herself to know when not to follow her male partner and leader blindly, and to step into her own leadership role by taking responsibility for her happiness in a way that saves everyone around her.

For her, being the flow of the water and playing the female role in the relationship, there comes a time when her feminine energy must evolve and integrate the masculine leading energy. During this time she will know when not to follow the leading male but to gain her independence instead. This happens when she becomes afraid and stops trusting her male partner. She now starts to direct her own flow of energy and when two masculine energies try to lead in different directions, it creates two separate focussed paths. Until she can appreciate his masculine leadership, she cannot surrender her own masculine direction. She cannot separate from you if she doesn't step into her independence. But she will also not grow beyond being the helpless victim. In the time that I became conscious of this, I found myself working with women in my coaching practice, workshops and mentor programmes who showed me this pattern.

Leading as the new feminine
When a woman recognises a man who can lead her, she'll follow him despite her past pain, but this time not as a helpless, innocent, virgin-stage woman. This time she too can step in and lead from inner strength when she needs to, rather than falling prey to self-serving agendas of males who would like to garner another status trophy or have someone to serve their patriarchal needs. When a woman finally accepts and integrates her own inner masculine she can accept her role in society again as the feminine being led by a strong male, discovering her own feminine leadership style. She has gained wisdom and her man is equally strong. By integrating her more compassionate style, she'll stop fighting with her inner masculine, and not surrender to it, but instead start to move with the energy instead of directing it. Her inner marriage of feminine and masculine will be reflected in her physical world.

Most of what is known about the feminine extends to the virgin and mother stages, but very little talks to the wise woman stage.

The previously suppressed feminine
Society tabooed women who thought for themselves a long time ago. Instead, intuitive women leaders were cast out by belief systems and they, in turn, went underground to develop their intuitive natural gifts. The real beauty in women is when their truth is reflected in the size of their hearts and their capacity to hold love and think for themselves. We can see this in Lady Dianna and Mother Theresa and so many women whose identities have lesser public profiles. I don't believe feminism is any better

than men submerging their feminine energy. The time for suppressing one gender over another is over; transparency begins with equality. The greatest gift I received from the absence of my biological father was that I couldn't live through his projection of me. I had to find my own roadmap of the masculine, which turned me to my ultimate male. This was something I projected onto God because I didn't trust a man. Until I recognised God in my struggle, I wanted me to pull myself out of the limitations of my mind and remind myself of what love really was. Remember, that there is a part of the journey where only your partner can go. You can only hold space for her in love. When she faces her biggest fears and lets go of everything that no longer belongs, she is left with the only important thing that remains. It is that very thing that gives us hope and makes us realise the answer we were looking for was there all along, waiting to be noticed.

Concluding thoughts

Every woman goes through a transformation beyond the childhood imprint of who she believed she was, when she lets go of the past. She experiences this as she moves from her adult-nurturing stage and into her wisdom phase. In fact, it is what informs her of her real purpose – to bring her spiritual gifts into this world. She can express this through accepting her nurturing role, leading in a feminine way and seeing herself through you every day as she lives life more intimately through her senses of sight, hearing and touch. Her journey will be triggered in a certain way and go through stages that dance with her own inner feminine and masculine, in which your relationship plays out the roles, until she accepts the parts of herself she was struggling with.

Chapter 18

Between the dream

And the reality I perceive

Consciously feeling the gap

Is what releases love from inside

And my finest hour

Created from desire to be free

Feeling the pain of birth and chaos

Allowing alignment of losses and gains

– My Finest Hour

The Shadow Side Of Her Basic Needs

Every woman has wounds from incomplete soul journeys. These become needs and fears that drives her behaviour from the subconscious. In conjunction with biological triggers and accompanying psychological growth, they can also be linked to energetic or spiritual lessons that are learned along the way. Events will seem to reappear until these needs are met. Even though your partner has experienced trigger events, like her first sexual experience, it doesn't mean she completed the lesson that was required for spiritual growth.

With each rite we conquer our internal demons. When a woman says she wants to go to Peru on a vision quest to go find herself for her 40th birthday, like I did, it's a clear sign that there is something going on inside her. Her life can either present her with an obstacle to overcome or she might create one.

*It is the challenges that women face
that lead to their wisdom.*

Each internal challenge allows us to integrate our lost parts as we discover them and they appear in stages of our life, according to tribal wisdom:
- Birth brings up anger
- Bleeding introduces greed
- Her first sexual experience allows her to overcome lust
- Marriage enables her to deal with her laziness or apathy to fill her own needs
- Parenthood brings envy
- Old age introduces gluttony and over-indulgence
- Death deals with personal pride

The purpose of symbolic events

Rituals serve as the physical processes that keep our emotions from overwhelming us. If we can project what we feel into an object or physical experience long enough, to reflect on the message we're presented with, we can grow from it. An initiation's purpose is growth and it follows a path. When you recognise where you are in this process, it helps to make sense of what is happening in order to take the next step.

It begins with a realisation-like thought that settles in: "I am now married." The body experiences it almost with a shock. A change has happened. We wanted to be somewhere, and now we are there.

The way you used to do things will no longer work now that you are married and things have to rearrange themselves. In the event that you didn't take this step to be married consciously, you'll be confused about its implications. Visualise being married as a pebble being dropped in a still pond. The pond is the way your world used to work without the pebble. Once the pebble drops it creates a ripple effect, just like realising you aren't married. Does the water on the surface still appear calm or has something changed? In the event that you didn't go into this marriage willingly (or consciously) you'll resist the responsibility of marriage on many levels. Being at this stage consciously means that you are able to look at it with the necessary clarity to understand what you have to learn. You need a strong will and perseverance to continue, or you may find yourself stuck here. This is the point where, if we don't participate and pursue the lesson, we keep repeating the same pattern and keep experiencing the same core events.

In the test phase, our emotions reveal our limiting beliefs about ourselves, and we have to master them in order to adjust to our new environment.

In the fourth and last part of the process she accepts that being single is now in the past and she steps into her true potential as a married woman. She has an understanding at the deepest level that satisfies her soul with her man. There is no need to be open to any other man when her partner is meeting her core need. Being tested and passing the test, she knows her substance beyond her role of being married.

Maybe this initiation should replace the wedding ceremonies that have become displays of our status and power. Without our knowledge, the soul consistently gives us opportunities to play this out in the drama of our lives. All we have to do is participate fully.

Challenges have a meaningful sequence

Although the biological life cycle creates an order of events for a woman to master the accompanying spiritual journey of her soul, she can still miss the moral lesson of the event after the biological triggers have come and gone. Her emotional drive becomes the signal for you to understand where and how you might be able to assist her, and to identify at what stage she is still incomplete. I would like to introduce benchmarks so that you may recognise, or help her to recognise, the obstacles that still stand in her way, from what I have discovered in Alberto Villoldo's work. He lived in South America on his own vision quests and for those who wish to learn to more about the demons we face on soul journeys I strongly recommend reading *Illumination: The Shaman's Way of Healing*.

Basic human needs are deeply seated in the psyche. If your partner cannot address them she will struggle with them until they are resolved, and it will impact on your relationship. Notice her strong and repetitive emotions and what they might indicate on a deeper level.

Anger masks inner acceptance

Through overcoming violent anger, in the physical process of birth, we may access our internal peace. The right to be born and to belong can create emotions of both anger and peace. Only your partner will know how deep and underpinned anger is in her internal reality. What you notice is like an iceberg, of which most is under the surface. Even if she is dealing physically with triggers that follow the logical order of biology, dealing with anger comes from the ritual of birth. Unresolved issues can still be the deep underlying motivator for her behaviour, completely unknown to her. As an umbilical cord is cut to symbolise detaching from the mother, if there are unresolved issues they will show up as an attachment she has with her mother and father's dreams, beliefs and fears. This implies that she takes on anger or sins that have been passed down by her parents in the family system. Without understanding, she is already open for resistance and experiences that create anger towards her parents and God. And we know that what she feels towards her parents will be projected onto her male partner when she starts her own family.

A successful rite of passage includes the parents' willingness to see their children as extensions of themselves. If they don't acknowledge her at birth she has to separate emotionally from her parents, or do everything according to what they tell her. The birth process to a baby is like going through a dark tunnel. To heal this we go through it metaphorically.

I understand now why I had a dream where I clearly said good-bye to five people I knew and loved just before I entered a dark cave at the same time my first husband was diagnosed with cancer. It earmarked the beginning of a destiny to discover what was mine to give to the world that would acknowledge my place in the world detached from my late husband and family.

Some disciplines will explain this anger as the amygdala hijacking the prefrontal lobes to prevent higher thinking, like reasoning, to takes place and override anger. When we don't recognise where we belong in our family system, we go into flight or fight mode, and we don't manage to stay calm when we encounter potential problems.

Other signs to look for are women who constantly need to prove themselves. Often a woman will take on a name of her own, which holds the dreams she defines for herself, through a spiritual name or a nickname. The significance of a name is related to how the woman sees herself. A married name still doesn't include her own identity as she sees herself. In native tribes the inclusion of the father's name shows the identity of the child as the whole being and completes integration, instead of choosing one name over another to replace it. Claiming her own is a signal that she will no longer hold others accountable for her choices.

Know that when your partner experiences this intense internal conflict that brings up anger, what she really seeks is inner peace. She needs to be able to understand that the anger she feels comes from energetic cords with her absent father or mother, because they were not *present* to welcome her into the world. Of course, this presence is referred to as emotional, physical, mental and energetic; the same way we desire to connect intimately to our partners. The way she'll stop trying to please her parents (or you, because it is transferred onto you) is by claiming her own dream and destiny in life and to accept herself completely. In a way she needs to give back to her parents, and others, the emotional stuff she took on that wasn't hers.

It helps to put healthy boundaries in place and say no, for her to love herself more and stop expecting you to nurture her. Allow her to rebel and express herself in order for her to hear herself. Use the medium of expression to heal her. This way, if you're completely present mentally and emotionally sensitive, she can really see and hear exactly what she needs to do to discover her own solution. By doing it this way, you show her the ultimate respect and love she really needs to find her own inner peace. This is what a woman really needs to be independent rather than being left to her own devices to discuss her overreacting emotions with her girlfriends and substitute a soul desire with financial independence. Substitutions eventually lead to her leaving you, because she doesn't know what else to do but to start over. All she will really create for herself, although she cannot understand it now, is temporary relief, because what she needs to heal will reappear in her life with other people.

When she cannot face her anger, she'll fall into the trap of self-abuse like so many women who impose on their relationships a distortion of perception, where they are consistently *done in* and they have someone else to blame. In this game of *victimhood*, she is the vulnerable victim of the story she tells herself. In every story, she experiences a victim and saviour. Authority cannot protect her and she cannot trust life because she cannot accept herself. She is a victim until she finds inner peace through acceptance to fill the emptiness of her soul.

How does she give? Is she generous or greedy?
One of the much-loved attributes of a radiant woman is her generosity. Her first period marks her joining the company of other women who share a mystical power to bleed without dying, as natives poetically describes it according to Villoldo.

There are many things that stand in the way of becoming emotionally and intellectually independent. There is no tribal ritual for urban living that symbolise the gift of women to the world. How can she be invited to take care of herself as a contributing woman? She is no longer a dependent child. Without her independence she will end up feeling controlled by men, substituting the parent role in her life. In Western society we don't go to the field to bury a cloth but we live in our parents' houses for longer than we need to, implying that we miss out on the wisdom and opportunity to become psychologically independent.

Womanhood has a unique value. If she completes the soul journey successfully, she'll give without losing her freedom in your relationship. She'll discover that to truly receive she needs to give without expectation and from a place of joy for *gifting*'s own sake. In fact, she'll have no secret need to be dependent on you. She knows how to take care of herself when required.

Because she knows her self-worth and is in charge of her own fertility and sexuality, she empowers herself. She won't give her power away in exchange for favours. She accepts her responsibilities in life as a woman with value. Even money comes into play here – an incomplete initiation results in scarcity *thinking*. She uses her sex appeal to seduce men for personal enrichment. Business is conducted without fully realising the implications, and is not focussed on an outcome where both parties benefit. Women develop a *what's-in-it-for-me* attitude. Feelings of inadequacy are never overcome and adult life remains an internally unhappy one. Instead of being a generous contributor to society, her focus is her own advancement and her personal agenda becomes impure.

Independence is created and a sense of purpose will be revealed when we have something of value to offer. This is one of the most important reasons I created platforms for women to explore their gifts in the world. Everyone has their own story of how they found out about their first menses and may not have had a way to complete this initiation.

If you want to assist her, ask your partner to tell you her story and listen carefully to how she feels emotionally. Notice what intellectual meaning she makes of it. Encourage her to share with you what her gift is in the world as she sees it, and explore ways to take it into the world and contribute to her community.

Substitute lust for closeness

Yes, as if I can hear your thoughts, I hear that question: "Oh, why do I want her to overcome lust?" Because, if your partner cannot convert her lust into purity through the initiation of her first sexual experience, she will never quite understand why she cannot experience intimacy to the extent that satisfies her soul. A huge percentage of women in my coaching office want intimacy more than anything else. There it is safe for them to tell me what you should hear as men. Intimacy includes passionate sex, love and connecting with you on all the levels she might have opened herself up to without any walls of separation.

For animals, intimacy is similar to grooming and it may have almost no association with sex at all. Humans and animals have separate meanings of intimacy. In many African tribal communities, women and men have an exploring stage to learn about their physical needs for intimacy, and when it's explored fully, they can move on to have perfectly healthy relationships where controlling sexuality is normal.

It's natural for men to notice and want many partners. One way to overcome drama repeating itself is to learn the spiritually underpinned lesson. Your relationship *is the right one*, but it's you who needs to become the right partner. Instead of searching for the right person, we need to shift our focus to ourselves.

For a woman to experience sensorial intimacy, she has to be able to lose control and surrender to her lover in orgasm and release oxytocin, a bonding hormone that intensifies her experiences of intimacy with her lover. These experiences go deeper each time. The brain centre that screens behaviour literally needs to shut down in order to let go of her inhibitions. On an emotional level she needs to trust her lover, to open up. There is a saying that a woman's legs open after her heart does and that for a man it works the other way around. A man who becomes the object of a woman's lust is right to be terrified of giving her intimacy. It just feels wrong. The natural sharing of joy, pleasure and intimacy requires a certain amount of emotional maturity. But for many women, the first sexual experience was rather painful and sex is not something that she can give herself to for pleasure, which amplifies her need to open emotionally first. This is often partly the result of a previous incomplete initiation of birth and first periods. It creates an energetic pattern where her willingness to allow you inside her comes with an expectation, which may become an attachment later.

The good news is that as we engage with our inner masculine and feminine energies, we're more able to learn about the art of giving and receiving. The bedroom becomes the stage where you can invite your partner to seduce you sexually and you can conquer her until she learns to give for joy. You can reverse roles and also add fantasy to the experience – of deep physical longing that welcomes all feelings to be present for her to heal. As inhibitions go and intimacy is increased, sharing together can create higher states of consciousness. The spiritual lesson here is to get to the place of pure intention where giving is generous and there are no more personal identities, but rather a partnership acceptance where one plus one equals more than two. She won't surrender only to you, but also to the spirit of your partnership. True intimacy is where man and woman merge into one soul beyond polarity.

To experience true intimacy one develops the purity of an innocent heart.

Is she lazy or courageous?

This brings us to the lesson of courage. Considering that at this stage we have learned the spiritual lessons of inner peace, generosity and purity, the soul needs of belonging, self-value and intimacy have been met. To have the courage to create a union with you before God, she needs to feel safe with you. Imagine her accepting you into her inner circle at the same level that she views herself before God. What she needs to take this step is commitment, for her to be that close to you at the stage of her life after learning the lessons of birth, her first period and sex.

Historically, women received meat for sex from pre-historic men. Past intimacy experiences were probably limited to marriages that were arranged to increase the status of tribes or families, or prevent wars.

Modern-day marriages are popular despite the divorce statistics, which demonstrates the number of times women are willing to get married and open their hearts for the right experience. Does this mean they are courageous? Modern women bring in their own *meat* and women rebel against being trophy wives. The usual patterns have been reset, as indicated by their capacity to provide for themselves and changing the rules of the traditional arrangement for female roles in relationships. What is even clearer is the lack of predefined boundaries of sacred marriage. Her laundry list might include a legal arrangement with full protection, emotional safety, non-stop romantic courting expectations, passionate sex in a happily-ever-after story, a best friend and full acceptance of her faults and a good sense of humour. She may even expect her man, by projecting her unhealed wounds onto him, to find the *solutions* that fix the problems she cannot express properly. If you cannot, she blames you for it. She wants the perfect partner despite her fears of intimacy, inadequacy and complete acceptance of herself.

Relationships are sparked by the needs we have and our partners' abilities to fulfil them. She expects you, as her life partner, to provide her solutions. She might lack the courage to conclude an agreement in the marriage, including her real needs, which will lock her into a state of apathy. What paralyses her is literally coming from an emptiness she is hoping you can fill, by projecting her unspoken fears onto you as her male partner. To be courageous, she needs to acknowledge and meet her unmet needs and become accountable. If necessary, this will include her previous core needs of:

Self-acceptance
Feelings of inadequacy
Fear of intimacy

The next step is to establish healthy, clear boundaries, for example "no meat, no sex" as was the need accepted previously. The needs that have to be met by both parties must be extremely clear.

Rules create the structure for the family system. What are shared in the partnership will become the goals for the newly created family, which lead to personal growth. For example, rules could include each partner's willingness to accept their responsibilities, once boundaries make the roles clear. The reward for a completed rite of passage is passion.

The bond of marriage is tested in many ways. The tests can include money, children or any challenge that threatens to bring out different agendas and individual needs; needs that override the partnership's sacred agreement. This will expose parts of the identity that are not integrated and open for self-healing. Unwillingness to co-operate and the courage to be accountable for your own decisions will indicate whether your partner has learnt the underlying lesson.

When you make a choice, will you take time to deal with this core need or have an intense discussion about what is important in the relationship for needs to be addressed? When she disappears into her own world and shows her reluctance to get involved, mental absence is as good as physical absence and a sign that she is not ready for commitment in marriage. With each withdrawal into herself, she heals a little more until the value of marriage gives her the courage to override her own needs with the commitment to both individuals' needs by accepting the responsibility that stands before her.

When the rite of passage has been fully integrated she is not defined by her marriage, nor is she in the partnership because she is scared of being single. She actually wants to be with her partner more than wanting to serve her own needs. If you realise that your partner is not ready to be passionate about your marriage, encourage her to set up a new written agreement where you both list what you bring into the partnership and what your core needs are. This may include things and responsibilities, but should also include gifting of values, that even if you have nothing or do nothing, you offer this just because you choose to. This is something you'll do because it's who you are, versus something that requires effort. It may even be something like gentle love. Let the agreement acknowledge what is hers to offer, especially if society doesn't value it.

Overcoming jealousy

When two identities are integrated into a union in marriage, the right to parenthood takes it to the next level, as compassion develops to include *others*. A woman's priorities shift from her personal values of what is important to what her children's needs are right now. When a couple put their needs aside to include those of a baby, the child becomes the teacher of values. A natural nurturing instinct takes over for her. Whatever is needed, the parent provides, no matter the cost, to the point that the child's needs come first.

There is a difference between being ready to make a child the focus of your life and wanting a child to be a perfect reflection of you. Let's look at an example with two women: one woman is ready for parenthood and the other woman needs to heal her childhood wounds. Certain elements are needed for parenthood to create an environment that is able to nourish and protect a child's needs. The environment two people provide needs to be safe and secure, with a firm structure. Rules are necessary to teach the child boundaries, and these will stem directly from the healthy boundaries that create the relationship bond they have.

A mother who is comfortable with herself can dedicate herself fully to her children, to assist them as they discover their own gifts, instead of being envious of their opportunity to live their dreams. The risk is that she, if not ready, will project her own unrealised dreams onto her children. How she brings her children up will be with the freedom to live their own lives or to extend herself through them. Compassion is needed to know the child's needs in order to nurture them. The better she can express and understand their needs, the more they'll be able to meet their own needs as they grow up and are free to live in independent relationships. Without developing compassion for herself, she'll make decisions to advance herself before the child as she puts her own unmet needs first.

Society has changed the status of children from having them for the benefit of the parents to being special and deserving of nurturing treatment. When they do overcome their jealousy, parents cannot wait for the day that children can give back to them. Again we can notice how parents give with strings attached. When parents do overcome envy, they have compassion, not just for their children, but everyone around them, as well as themselves. We learn through our children. I'm not sure any parent is ever ready for children before the baby arrives. As our kids grow through certain ages, we relive our own experiences reflected to us at those ages in order to be given another chance to heal them.

Overindulgence or wisdom

Evolution teaches us that humans have evolved further than surviving animals as a species, through discovering wisdom. In the marshmallow experiment we discover that impulse control brings more success. Old age introduces wisdom as a rite of passage to bring maturity to childish needs. Even children have to develop certain wisdom as a new baby arrives in a family and the parents focus their attention on the new arrival. If the child cannot develop this wisdom, he or she becomes the daddy's girl who never grows up and always needs his attention to acknowledge her needs. Society and business reward us with success if we act according to the accepted values of the masses, which don't always represent wisdom.

Female sages are the visionaries of society. They see opportunities when others see problems. We live in an information age, not a wise society. We are *not required to think for ourselves.* We are not rewarded for asking questions. A wise woman is recognised when she is no longer in competition with younger beautiful women, but chooses to mentor them and share her knowledge freely. Symbolically, the daddy's princess now becomes queenly, and gives up the role of drama queen. Instead of replacing her role as mother or innocent virgin, a woman includes all of these roles. She shifts her need for building wealth to making a contribution to her world. She is constantly discovering her value. She is clear about what she wants to do and allows others to influence her for the betterment of humankind. To go through this initiation, she experiences the *dragonfly transformation* that leads to nurturing and intimacy skills, standing in her leadership role and understanding the world as a reflection of her interior journey.

Pride

The initiation of death brings the experience of true humility as humans and reminds us that we are but small players in the bigger scheme of things. Death can also be attempted mythically through a process that will separate consciousness from the body and the identity of self. There are many shamanic ways that guide these experiences like taking mushrooms or regression soul journeys. In Egypt, pharaohs were put in sarcophaguses until their souls left their bodies and revived again to gain this wisdom before they were given the throne.

Today, we remember our mortality and some of us have direct encounters beyond what we know as earthly things. Experiencing this allows us to increase our wisdom and power so much more. For me these came through feeling alive as I tested the boundaries of reality and lived on the edge. These experiences remind us that we're human and alive. But not everyone wants to walk on fire, jump out of aeroplanes or swim in the sea alone for hours after they almost drowned as a child, to overcome their fears. A successful initiate is recognised by their smile when someone attacks their ego. They are able to separate who they believe they are from their *earth identity* completely. There is little need to show the world you are important so you use your energy for what matters. Finally, accept that we have to trust life as a teacher and let go of our fears, knowing how small we are as our pride dissolves in daily life. Recognising your partner's biggest obstacles before she does, leads her to engage with her life's experiences, which encourages her to deal with her internal challenges one by one. Remember previous incomplete lessons impact on the ones that are still to come.

Concluding questions

There is value in understanding at what stage of your partner's journey your reflections may bring her awareness, gently. Asking some of the following questions may guide you closer to understanding which spiritual lessons she is learning:
- Does she experience any of the following emotions frequently: anger, greed, lust, jealousy, over-indulgence or pride?
- Is she able to acknowledge her core needs for belonging, being enough, being valued, being completely open and trusting, commit to responsibility, and being compassionate and humble?

Notice the level at which your partner's inner struggle might be triggered. Allow her to express and learn by being a soundboard to face the stage of personal growth she finds herself in.

Chapter 19

When we remember

You will recognise the path everywhere

In the trees and water and sunshine

And we will feel it in our hearts

Give permission to feel

To touch your own emotions

And your soul will yearn for completion

When you are, will you remember?

– A Path to Remembering

Finding Herself

Finding herself recovers the lost femininity in all women (or men) as they experience the triggers in life that call them inward. Allow me to repeat that the feminine referred to here is the internal feminine side all men and women have, not just women, but for the purpose of the book I will refer to women's development.

Rejecting parts of ourselves

Every woman meets her inner feminine on her inward journey. How much she accepts or rejects of herself (her inner feminine and masculine) is reflected in her external world through her relationships. If she chooses to reject or judge someone, she's really judging or blaming a part of herself that she cannot yet accept, as I have repeatedly pointed out.

Finding herself again starts with the imprint she receives from her parents as she grows up. It forms her expectations of her own relationship. Are her parents alive or dead? What *mental* maps does she have of her mother and father? If one of her parents was absent, she has a longing for a map that reflects that part of herself as the masculine or feminine. If a substitute parent was present, they may *symbolise* the relationship with the shadow of that missing parent.

If your partner had an absent parent, she'll be psychologically deprived of the feeling of acceptance of what the absent parent stands for in herself, as her masculine or feminine. It is exactly this parent deprivation that might trigger her inward journey at some point.

By now you'll realise that the *feminine story* is a turning inwards in her self-development focus. By turning inwards I mean feeling the pain that drives her behaviour in order to heal through acknowledgment and acceptance. In the relationship, this is first experienced through you and then through herself.

The influence of conditioned learning

A major event, like death or a normal cycle that she enters in her life, starts her journey inwards into the unconscious world and drives her behaviour. To turn inwards implies acquiring the necessary knowledge of ourselves to learn to reclaim our projecttions.

The inner masculine and feminine recognise themselves as reflections of our parents from a deep place within us that goes way beyond our conditioned learning of the roles we are taught. Conditioned learning applies to the outside world's view of reality, but inside us we are *remapping* what we might remember or recognise from a much deeper place.

On a physical level, a woman experiences her inner feminine more easily when balanced by the masculine in her partner in the external world, as she dances with the polarity within herself.

Ignorance of the inner connection

As if a mystical presence visits us in a special dream (or the experience of death of a loved one), we are invited to wake up in the subconscious mind. What was clear to us during these deep internal moments of feeling connected to ourselves, we cannot be sure about when we are being logical and physically awake. The experience of ourselves in this *subconscious* feels like a state between dreaming and being awake, as if we can almost retain the memory but not quite, because what we remember of it doesn't add up logically. Mentally, during these deep moments of recognition of the feminine, the brain lights up with pleasure hormones that leave a sense of purity and perfection similar to a-ha moments when some insight comes to us. For me, remembering these moments of insight are possible because I associate them with the dragonfly experiences.

Engaging with daily experiences of life and listening to what people say to us from *outside* disconnects us from our internal experiences and we forget about the things that don't make sense in our *normal* world.

If we choose to ignore the invitations to go within, our unmet soul need will keep driving our behaviour toward the unconscious, and our behaviour might become irrational as we deal with normal daily events. As we choose to forget about our soul moments because they don't fit in our conditioned understanding of how the world works, the *normal* world might stop making sense to us until we go on the journey inwards to the *only place where our irrational behaviour might make sense to us.*

In relationships, these shadows come out as we trigger the pain and unhealed wounds that control our behaviour from the background. In order to face the shadow and heal, we need to feel again, and as we feel we start to take back control as we learn to nurture our core needs. Not participating, or choosing not to feel the pain, distorts the experience of love for power as we attribute incorrect meanings to events.

Participating on the inward journey allows our self to absorb the pain of an unlived life with a missing parent or correct an incorrect meaning from a past painful event. With a *healthy* map of her inner feminine, this connection with the subconscious will provide her with the process to heal herself.

Unlearning conditioned behaviour: Revealing the inner feminine

It is important here to recognise that a woman's own real voice is not that of her substitute mother or her mother, but her own inner feminine, which is loving and kind. She discovers it inside on her soul journey into the subconscious. Notice how many of her mother's behaviours she copies. Does she act like her mother? To overcome the map of the feminine that was passed down from her mother, she needs to be strong enough within herself to tell the imposing mother-voice in her mind that guides her behaviour through conditioning to go away. In time, she'll learn that this voice of her mother doesn't belong to her either, nor does the voice of her grandmother. It belongs to whomever she decided to believe about who she is. As she grew up, her mother's instructions guided her to accept or reject behaviour through reward or punishment. Her appropriate behaviour created her self-identity based on her mother's map passed down by her grandmother. At some point, the soul journey invites her to decide for herself who she wants to be and to discover parts of herself that her conditioning deprives her of. These *discovered parts* are often the keys to your relationship with her. As she discovers and accepts these parts, her acceptance of you as you reflect these to her, will bring harmony and intimacy into the relationship. The judgements that were accepted, and that bonded them over eons of time as a collective, are passed down through parenting. As she discovers this she can give what was not hers back to her parents and free herself to live authentically and without projections.

The inner feminine journey is often misled and delayed when women are abused or fall into depressions and struggle their way through addictions, because this keeps them unconscious about what is really needed at a soul level. If you notice any self-destructive behaviour in your partner, it's useful to know that this only masks her deep desire to connect with herself.

Living unconsciously makes it hard to meet the divine within when the necessities of our physical existence require all our focus and attention. Can we truly stay in touch with our feminine in unconscious relationships? And for how long? Do we understand the drive to go within? Is this emptiness we feel not a clue that what we're trying to do is never going to work until we accept that this is a soul desire that needs to be met within at a soul level?

As children we feel a sense that something amazing is going to happen to us. Some of us can even remember something about experiences that makes us believe we are special with a special purpose. We want so much to believe that people will acknowledge us for this *ability*, not realising that the magic is inside and outside. We forget and the something we waited for never happens. Reconnecting inside brings so much clarity in our lives during these times.

I have a recurring dream when things get too hectic for me. In my dream, I am a soul chained to a wall with many chains from which I easily break free. I usually wake up knowing all will be well no matter how impossible it seems in my logical world, but it leaves me with an inner knowing I have learned to trust. This is what knowing ourselves in the subconscious brings. It brings intuition and a voice we can trust, even when nothing about it seems logical. We eventually have to accept that we live an ordinary life but the magic is inside. Or we fight for an ideal cause bigger than us, like equality, but eventually give up because we have to make the best of what we have and give up on the promise that our ideal world cannot be.

If we don't have a suitable frame of reference at the time that something amazing happens, we'll forget it and it remains unconscious, just like not having a dragonfly story to associate it with.

The imprint of the divine experience stays in the psyche of a woman and this becomes the drive behind her seeking what is missing in her life later on, as it was for me when I went on my vision quest to try to connect what I felt but could not remember.

Recognising the feminine

I can recall sitting on the toilet as a seven-year old. I used to take all my clothes off for some odd reason, and I would measure my growth against the sides of the toilet seat (a really peculiar habit). I was quite skinny and had to balance myself by holding my hands on the back of the toilet seat.

My parents had many cats. If one particular black cat stood in the doorway, I would escape through the toilet window with no clothes on. I remember one day, as I sat on the loo kicking my legs against the wall in a daydream state. I thought that the wall was *not solid*. I was moving my foot right through the wall. Was it my imagination? I cannot remember.

I do remember getting to high school where the chemistry teacher told us that everything is made of atoms that move all the time. Well that day I thought I was pretty smart, because I already knew that at half that age. The significance to me was that I already realised *internally* that I could trust what I *knew* by what informed me from *inside*. This was probably my first introduction to recognising the inner feminine.

It is human nature to avoid pain and seek pleasure

Our need for predictable behaviour destroys our imagination. The education system and the media tell us what and how to think, to spare us from having to think for ourselves. In one company I worked for, we were told exactly how to think through step-by-step rules, and every fibre in my being objected. Humans become more lazy and unconscious. Futurists said the biggest skill of the 21st century would be to unlearn. Books like Eckhart Tolle's *Now* or *A New Earth* became famous for teaching us to be present in the moment. Did we lose our ability to deal with the intensity of spirit and replace it with repetitive TV? We know life by what we are told through advertising and media, without having to think for ourselves. Why are there so many magazines today? Why do people prefer to look outside themselves for what informs them?

This speaks to our demons of unmet need for belonging, and having a partner to meet our needs and help us with self-acceptance.

On the journey of the feminine, we start to think for ourselves again. At some point, the masculine also joins in as we connect inside to a universal sense of logical laws. We discover the natural laws that drive our humanity beyond our beliefs.

If we go deep enough we realise that pleasure is short-lived and sometimes it is engaging with the pain we avoid at all costs, which rewards us by serving the soul.

Unlearning conditioned projections

When we are conscious, we remember and recognise what we have lost. There is always something left behind to give us a starting place from which to find what the soul needs, and it is often in the pain we resist feeling. The Divine informs us through intuition how to meet our inner feminine one step at a time. I believe that at this stage women realise that this deep internal connection first has to be met by themselves before they can meet their partners here in this space. As they heal within, it's reflected through their external relationship with you. Her automatic responses will change to become conscious decisions until they too become set constructive habits. However, that is easier said than done. When she realises how it works, she will find a willing partner with whom she can project her deepest internal desires and find more of her lost parts consciously. This is different to just expecting you to do for her what she cannot do for herself and projecting unconsciously. Projections cannot be avoided, but we can witness them as we do them, which lessens blaming her partner, you.

Moving deeper into the feminine: Getting to know ourselves
When I needed to find myself I literally felt *called* to visit Peru to connect with that part of divinity inside myself. There were no neon signs, just a dream and a deep desire to visit a place, on a continent I knew nothing about. I had no idea what it was about.

Maybe for me that was my first exploration, actively searching for the divine within to find what was missing inside me, alone.

The shadow side (the unacknowledged feminine) becomes part of the process to help us connect with our pain.

We go into the subconscious where nothing seems familiar to us and all meanings seem to be the opposite of what are in the *real* world. This ritual talks to our wounds and takes away set ideas we have about ourselves. To participate in this journey consciously, we must dedicate time and focus to create the mind-space where we can start making different decisions. We need to challenge ourselves to change habits and create the changes we want, based on how well we know ourselves now, and heal the pain that drove us there originally. The pain might stem from the joy felt during our initial intimate experience of real love when we had a brief mystical experience or it might come from a longing for absent parents. We rejected our absent parents because we refused to see ourselves as abandoned, so we also rejected that part within our own masculine or feminine, but now we want it back. To heal we go underground to the negative emotion, to transform it into something constructive. This is not a once-off journey and might take many years of effort.

Every coin has two sides. Marian Woodman describes the inner feminine as both the nurturing mother and the ruthless hunter who feeds her cubs. We would be mistaken to assume the feminine purpose is only to bring us food to grow. She does what she has to do or none of us would survive, and now she also has to *turn within* to become complete and emerge on the outside with her own voice.

Do you ever feel she is testing you?
The female teases the masculine with her lessons as our intuition is tested by logic. The female shadow has a question: *"Why are you here?"* The female's authenticity (how well she now knows herself) and accountability for her previous actions (if she can pull her projections back) that caused her pain will be tested. Her intentions must show her purpose clearly to grow into the next stage of trust. She needs to *own* her shadow, meaning that she needs to recognise her participation that created the emotions that she blames others for. In the relationship, this is reflected when your partner creates the environment that will test your purpose, and if you are strong enough she will follow you. In her inner world she will take back her power as she realises that the resources she needs to heal her pain are hidden within her own suppressed fears.

Real life distracts her mind-space with practicalities to survive: eating, creating income and shelter, and she shows her commitment to the journey when she has to find a way to do this as well as meet her basic needs. The material world's daily challenges now need to be aligned with our spiritual integrity, and we need to *do* what we say and think about, in order to live authentically.

Her beliefs, and frame of reference, need to adjust as she speaks from her heart, and this becomes her personal contribution as she emerges in her new feminine. To pass the tests, she integrates both the logical and illogical.

Giving the feminine boundaries
She needs to learn to value herself. She navigates the subconscious in the hope of rediscovering divinity inside herself. The next search

takes some time and teaches her about self-love. The pain of the journey to find what she was looking for shows her how much the self was not appreciated until now.

The feminine not only discovers how much she did not love herself, but is also reflected through her relationship with you and her vocation. Until she discovers love for herself, she cannot recognise her capacity to feel compassion for other people. For example, she might treat people as objects, or treat her career with the same nurturing as she would treat people. If she nurtures her career as if it is a person, she probably rejects her feminine and accepts her masculine in the way that she connects to the world through her work. She will create distance between herself and people if her feminine is hurt or disconnected, and take on careers like law, engineering, science or any career that allows her to distance herself from the soft and warm experience of compassion with humans.

Our office spaces reflect the distance we create between ourselves and other people. Looking at our naked bodies and the taboo society places on exhibiting sensuality, reminds us of our previous wounds of lost freedom to be as we were born, in naked innocence.

The walls come down so all that is left is transparency. The longer a woman stays in the underworld of negative emotions, the bigger her voice becomes, and when she comes back her voice has to be listened to. Reasoning with our own shadow makes us stronger than we were and allows us to break out of the unconscious field.

Choosing the inner feminine to lead her
The breakthrough comes when the feminine's internal journey makes the choice to return to the external world from her inner quest. Her dreams of flying are reflective of this journey in the spiritual world. She can return from depression when she is strong enough on the inside to emerge and express herself clearly with the

power she claims as she stands up for what she believes. Sometimes the female doesn't look directly at her wounds, for fear for being overwhelmed by them.

She conveniently forgets about her divine interventions, marries for advantage rather than love, and in doing so she is not true to herself, but does what she has been taught to value.

Can she listen to the power of feeling in her own heart? In the subconscious underworld, sound as feeling cannot deceive her in the same way that information does, represented as light. She recognises her intentions with the language of resonance and her own intuition.

Maybe her only way out of being stuck in the negative emotions is to feel. The substance of the universe is sound and light, and to hear sound means to listen with her heart. Feelings can be difficult to trust, because they don't seem logical.

By letting go of taught concepts of what is accepted in society from a woman, and her previous role, she now identifies with a clear purpose, which allows her to feel again.

Feeling the pain

Not every woman accepts the invitation to become conscious on her search for the Divine. When I chose to leave my ex-husband and express myself for who I was, I was also discarded by those in my family who chose not to make the same decisions and limited themselves to the decisions made by others of how they were allowed to express themselves. It was not the men, but the women who reacted the most. In *Eat, Pray, Love* Liz Gilbert's best friend has to stay behind with her baby and husband while Liz fulfils her inner craving to find her mojo. Liz's friend reveals that she wished it had been her instead.

We need *a voice* to experience an inner purification, loud enough to reason with our own shadow and find our purpose.

Anatomy of emotions

To feel can be painful. What she feels can be explained by what neuroscience now teaches us about emotions. What she feels will be interpreted through memories and then reconstructed in order to rearrange her logic to meet her intuition. It is her memory that explains her behaviour. How we put our stories together is what limits or liberates our emotions. Meanings can distort our experience and limit our vision of our own truth versus the facts.

Negative emotions tell us she is already highly stressed. If we ask her to feel the raw emotions beyond her story again, the story of her trauma (or repetitive chronic pain, which is the body's map) releases stress hormones through old neurological pathways of the fight or flight response. She is now highly sensitive about what might trigger overwhelm in her internal feeling world.

Most women who have dealt with trauma or excessive emotional baggage develop coping skills that enable them to desensitise. But being desensitised in order to deal with life, for the purpose of finding her lost and rejected self, doesn't serve her.

The personal risk she takes to seek out her feminine is possibly the most stressful thing she has done and leaves her vulnerable and, from the outside, irrational.

She overreacts easily to the outside world. The stress hormones also weaken her memory where it is situated in the hippocampus.

Up to the age of three, feelings are stored in the amygdala (our reptilian brain) mostly without memory. The hippocampus stores feelings in relation to context memories. When expected to feel (to heal old wounds) what was previously ignored (as a coping skill to protect us because it was possibly inappropriate to feel at the time), it is important to access resourceful hormones that can counter the stress hormones of feeling the pain. Stored memories delete factual information, or amplify it in the presence of cortisol and adrenaline when we bank memories. This incomplete storing of information under stress creates the distortions in the mind that leave us with half-truths about ourselves. Neuroscience tells us how informational memory is weakened, while emotional memory amplifies when stress hormones like adrenaline and cortisol are present.

As women now re-experience certain triggers for these emotions, their internal wiring overreacts compared to the actual threat in the external world, leaving them feeling even more misunderstood than before. From the outside, this seems irrational. But retelling the same story resets the emotions when the facts are logically considered and new emotions can be linked to the neurological pathway. We also need to remember that the fight or flight response is to put us into a state of alertness to protect us. But if these stress hormones are triggered outside of a physical danger, the energy that was summoned needs to be dispersed or it will surely show up as anger or anxiety and be inappropriately *banked* with these memories in the mind. We also have to remember that it is not the feelings themselves that are the enemy, but how we learn to cope behaviourally with those unhealed emotions. To allow feeling is a big part of the healing, without having to provide understanding.

As her partner, your biggest role is to witness her feeling her own emotions, and the more you show her how to have self-compassion, the less she will become dependent on you.

When she can reconnect with her feelings, she also reconnects with the self that she abandoned so long ago. The psychological inner journey is the capacity to communicate between the inner feeling child, the acting-out child (behaviour) and the adult who tries to protect the identity from understanding itself. And just like little children, they have to be taught to seek attention in healthy ways.

What does finding herself mean?

- Some painful event will trigger her to find her lost parts.
- The lost feminine is the part of herself that she rejected as a child.
- She blames you for what she cannot accept inside herself as you reflect it to her.
- She misses the part of herself that she rejected and, being frustrated with you, she turns inwards to find it.
- To navigate inside herself, she has to feel.
- What blocks her from finding what she cannot see, are her beliefs and taught behaviours about how the world works.
- She needs to find the courage to un-believe all she knows and *see the world upside down* through feeling.
- The stories that she told herself blocked her from feeling her pain, which is what she needs to feel again if she is going to find herself.
- She has to give up the coping skills she used to protect her from feeling.

- As she faces her past pain, she can choose to re-link the memories with the emotions, which she is now more equipped to handle.
- She creates new meanings of past events.
- She is more resourceful and brings intuitive feelings and the logic of facts together in a way that allows her express herself through a new story of who she knows she is.
- The new emerging feminine is not a taught identity through conditioning, but sees her own shadow and accepts her pain.
- When she emerges from the subconscious world, she has a new voice.

PART FOUR

What You Can Do To Assist

Her Transformation

Chapter 20

And you let it all out

Into the abyss

Into the place of transmutation

Then you look inside of you

And find that you have depth

More dimensions than you can imagine

Inside waves of sensations and feelings

Every emotion stronger than before

Deeper and raw

– Sometimes Depth Comes from the Lightness of Being

How Can She Be Taught To Nurture Herself?

The only way to help your partner to nurture herself is by supporting her with encouragement through behaviour. The simple story of giving a fish versus teaching another how to fish for herself demonstrates this. It does take longer to teach someone fishing instead of just feeding them. The recipient may even prefer not to learn how to fish and just get the fish, but then they will never learn how to help themselves.

In essence, women open to receive and men penetrate as they give to her. If she accepts this, you will repeat the action of giving. Napoleon Hill in *Think and Grow Rich* wrote this in 1937 as the attraction of the male and female exchange. In contrast to the masculine giving essence the female anatomy is geared to nurture the young. Physically, women appear as the vulnerable gender as well as being seen as the natural nurturers in society because of their softness and sensitivity in comparison with males.

Who takes care of the nurturers? When males gift females, women expect males to provide their nurturing in return, but at the point where her journey turns inwards he is ill-equipped to give her what she needs. She might not yet have discovered what is hers to contribute as the feminine. What happens now is that she receives from him until the time comes for her to know her own power of giving, from within herself. Ironically, in order to nurture others, she learns to nurture herself first. There is trouble in paradise when she *expects* you to nurture her all the time without learning that she can do this for herself.

I often observe how sorry women feel for themselves and how they blame their providers for not providing what they really need – intimacy. As a coach, I had to choose between giving them the nurturing they are unable to give themselves, or holding space for them until they figure out that they can do this for themselves. The how is the difficult part, because we are all unique. What works with one person doesn't work with another, because the focus is not on the external behaviour but rather the inner realisations that provide self-nurturing.

At this stage the relationship is taking on a direction that can feed fish or teach fishing. The behaviour we choose (to nurture or hold space) for her to learn to nurture her own needs, creates one of the games women play, where their vulnerability invites a hero to save them. She exchanges favours, the second biggest currency next to money, to gain perceived power. If her vulnerability is witnessed and held in reverence, she can be taught how to fish. Think of it as walking through a maze like a rat. Until it finally reaches the cheese, it keeps repeating the pattern for this to become a learned behaviour. If you choose not to nurture your partner, instead giving her the opportunity to discover what she needs, express it and do it for herself, she will feel what she really needs – self acceptance. There is nothing wrong with being connected to our inner child and feeling vulnerable, as long as we don't expect others to feel sorry for us. When you cry, the difference between being a victim and being self-nurturing is that the victim wants someone else to make them feel better, whereas the self-nurturer cries because they need to feel.

When my partner told me he was spoiling himself with a massage I don't even know where to begin to explain my internal resistance towards his selfishness. I questioned this within and was guided by another question: "If you could love you that much..?" So if I didn't have the capacity to allow self-nurturing, I don't allow it for others either. This resistance was, of course, my stuff and reflected how I wasn't giving myself permission to be nurtured in the way he was allowing himself to be nurtured. It was as if, compared to him, someone took my permission away. And now I didn't want my partner to experience what I didn't allow for myself. The remedy was to pull my projections back and recognise that what I really felt was nurturing myself in that way.

The hardest thing to understand when learning how to nurture, is that no one can ultimately teach us how to do it. We try different things and see how they make us feel. In the process, we discover how nurturing is experienced and repeat the feelings of being nurtured for ourselves. When a child is heartbroken, we know what to say to allow him or her to feel what they need to in order to nurture him or herself and grow to become emotionally literate. Giving a baby a dummy or food when they cry teaches them to become adults who fill the need for nurturing with comfort food and other things that help us to forget, like other coping skills do.

The difference between the real and the substituted need can be explained as follows: You can take a car apart and put it back together and it will go again. But you cannot cut a living body up and stitch it back together and expect it to live again. Nurturing has a special internal relationship with our souls. It is not a mechanical thing we do. You can do everything right, but your partner might still not feel nurtured. She needs to give permission to herself to accept the nurturing you give her. There are, however, some useful insights for you to know, when it comes to nurturing.

Differentiate between self-love and being a victim

The difference between being a victim and self-nurturing is shown in how we use our vulnerability for manipulating people to feel sorry for us. Caring for ourselves is no different to being willing to mother ourselves. Think of what it means to be a mom. Think of how your mother taught you to nurture yourself or what you learnt through what she didn't teach you. To stand in the feminine fully, you might have guessed, we need to heal our issues with our own mothers.

Assisting your partner with her nurturing needs means that you can choose to develop the skill to nurture your partner, knowing when to pull back so you don't create a codependence as you support her, or you can assist your partner in nurturing herself.

Dr Whitfield who wrote *Healing the Inner Child* said that in his 20 years of practice, he had never found a couple where two individuals nurtured each other.

Normally one person in the relationship is being nurtured while the other goes outside the relationship for their nurturing to a mother, sister or friend.

When we experience this one-way nurturing, it's easy for one partner to develop a game to get attention. The cost of creating a codependent relationship with which to nurture our partners is giving up sexual polarity in the long term. The polarity of gender that creates sexual attraction is risked at the cost of having a parent-child relationship. So it might be preferable to have an interdependent relationship and witness your partner nurturing herself, and it is useful to know how to encourage that.

Nurturing requires emotional sensitivity

To support your partner in nurturing herself starts with being emotionally sensitive enough to hear her unspoken needs and to notice when she might need nurturing. Help her to express her needs as she discovers them. Women don't know what they need. In part, this is why they get so angry when you don't know what they need, as this lack of knowing is projected onto you. You are the one she expects to nurture her needs, until this perception is corrected through your behaviour. All she knows is how you made her feel when she recognised herself in you, and she craves this feeling. What might appear obvious to you is not obvious to her. If you pull back your support in the way you normally provide it, by maybe doing what she needs, she will experience your withdrawal with separation anxiety.

Become sensitive to the emotions that are still very hard for her to understand and encourage her to express them, even if they don't appear to be positive. Encourage her to act on her own needs and remind her that she is worth it.

Teach her to take care of her own needs before those of the family, to create a more harmonious and happier space for everyone in the long term.

A woman who gives from an empty space is not as giving as a woman who gives with a fully recharged battery, nor does she resent giving what she herself needs to survive. Often women who deprive themselves of nurturing are unfulfilled mothers who attract partners they hope will fill the void inside them. But expecting her partner, you, to nurture her will only result in resentment towards you later on. When she does step into her feminine, you will need to be in your masculine, and directive.

Ultimately, as she explores her inner world, she will become her feminine self and need you to be her opposite and equal masculine to take the partnership to the next conscious level of engagement.

Dealing with her own mother

Encourage her to focus on the bond with her own mother to get the most appropriate nurturing. The biggest gift of motherhood is the deep spiritual lesson that we learn to love ourselves first. To understand this, we learn that what we resist in our mothers we also reject in ourselves, and we need to accept our rejected traits if we wish to heal.

When mother issues are healed, your partner can give and receive in a way that creates a healthy activation of sexual pleasure and love, as she experiences her inner parent and her inner child at appropriate times, to role play and express all of who she is.

Allow her to express her experience of her mother with you. Notice her allegiance and know that what she rejects in her mother, she rejects in herself. As she learns to accept these parts of herself, her issues with her mother will heal and her own feminine will mature. Does she stand up for herself, or does she do what her mother tells her to, and why? These observations can give her wonderful insights if discussed with compassion and good listening skills. Allow her to be herself without being prescriptive. She will ask for your input when she wants it. Always remember that awareness can be painful to the receiver. Give her lots of appreciation for her courage.

We nurture what we value

When you treat someone else with more importance than they treat themselves, you value them more than they value themselves. Notice how you feel treated. If you don't appreciate someone's behaviour, you'll draw on boundaries and express your needs clearly. If someone doesn't treat someone else equally, it's because this person allows it based on how they value themselves. Nurturing can truly be given to others when we can give it to ourselves, and has a lot to do with how we value the self.

> *Getting someone to save us as victims is not nurturing, it is a game of power and control.*

In order to self-nurture, we need to feel we are valuable enough inside ourselves. Respect and equality are not qualities that are abundantly available in society – we carry them inside of us, and claim from others as we give to them. So a valuable gift you can give your partner is to let her know in how many ways you find her beautiful. Hold the intention in the field for her to learn how to love herself: to self-care inside and out.

A woman who can nurture herself loves a man, despite the fact that he might die from cancer or drop her when the chips are down. A woman who nurtures her own needs chooses to give her heart freely. Such a woman knows that only she can save herself by accepting what she resists so much in you and others' reflections of herself.

> *She understands her own value and trusts her ability to nurture herself when she needs nurturing.*

We value what we can accept

A woman learns that true power is her ability to not *expect* anything from her partner, but to trust that what she needs will become available to her in order to take care of herself. When she is gifted with her own contribution she appreciates it. She can receive the male gaze that penetrates her very soul without feeling the need to offer a favour in return. She recognises the love that is already alive inside herself. She accepted herself and her clay feet a long time ago, and appreciates where she comes from. She is in awe of every day and its ability to rebirth a sunrise. She becomes nature and shines brightly for all to see. She shows her beauty to the world. She gifts her man with all of her body and the mirror of her soul. Love accepts him in totality with his challenges and opportunities. Love appreciates that in every moment it will witness what needs to happen and support it. Love knows that what is needed is exactly what will be. The sun will set when the day is done and all is perfect. She feels exhausted but fulfilled.

Love is so very pure in its essence to stay undefined and gives birth to many experiences to attempt to explain what it creates. It radiates from her being, both innocent and full of expression. Love is exactly all of that – the movement between two polarities for creation's sake. It asks only to be seen and heard as it expresses more of itself and it is so very beautiful in all its forms. Can she accept herself as all of that and value that?

Rejection teaches us to love ourselves more

One of my biggest lessons was to overcome my abuse as a young girl. I felt exceptionally vulnerable. I met a man at 17 who not only saved me, but helped me to feel safe. When that enabled me to know and understand how to feel safe enough to open like a flower and reveal my beauty, I didn't take the next step to learn to take care of myself. I still expected a man to keep me safe. Because I was not ready, I never figured out I could do it for myself.

Nurturing is not about feeling good because we're taking care of ourselves. We nurture deep-seated vulnerability when we risk feeling violated as women on emotional, sexual and intellectual levels and our boundaries are stepped on. Since a man loved me enough for me to feel safe to come out of my shell, I relied on that person to do it for me every time. Then the worst thing happened – he was taken away from me and I became a widow. For all my money and beauty, I would withdraw whenever I felt at risk and unsupported in my environment. And I felt at risk every time I liked someone, because I could be abandoned again. I made the safest decision I could. Life keeps presenting us with challenges to overcome our core imprint. Mine was to overcome feeling violated. The key was to face my own shadow and risk life, but instead I took the choice to escape the risk and be safe. It took me a long time to realise that I gave my power away to my late husband. As much as I loved him, I never realised I needed to nurture my basic need. I had to understand that when I knew what it felt like to be safe, I could just make the choice to be safe within myself. The worst thing that could happen had already happened to me and I survived it. Even when there was no real threat, my internal wiring had me feel unsafe every time I felt closeness. Having my own children's love was almost unbearable at the time. What I wanted so much, to experience myself through others, left me withdrawing because I was inappropriately scared that I would be abandoned again. It could all have been overcome if I had accepted love and nurturing.

Instead of realising all this, I married again to have a man protect me from feeling unsafe when it should have been as simple as realising I was already safe inside myself. Patterns keep repeating themselves until we get the spiritual lesson behind them. The neurochemistry in my neural network was so warped that I acted out each time my lack of receiving nurturing was triggered. I, like so many other scared women, made a safe and reasonable choice. Of course, this didn't mean I didn't love him, because we love everyone as much as we love ourselves. But it did mean that I got married to feel safe. And it also meant that I cut myself off from my own emotions. So did I accept my own emotions? What was my capacity to nurture myself? How vulnerable did I really feel and how did I handle it? The lesson of abandonment is that of rejection. The more our story reflects rejection, the more room we have to love ourselves instead of expecting others to do it for us.

Loving myself allowed me to reveal my own beauty.

Understanding the value of rejection teaches us how many of our life's lessons revolve around knowing ourselves as love. The more we know ourselves as love, the more our capacity to love our partners increases.

We keep repeating the same experiences until we learn from them

After the divorce my ex-husband told me that he felt betrayed. This was hard for me to understand, until I sat down quietly and wrote a letter to my late (first) husband, I couldn't understand that so long ago I gave the *power that protected me* to him. So in my letter I asked for it back, because I needed it, and finally I could let him go in peace. I was repeating the same pattern by giving away my power to feel safe to men. This applies to every person who, for whatever reason, doesn't know how to feel safe. When we tell ourselves someone else has this power to make us feel safe, it's a lie. The true power to feel safe is inside us. It is our willingness to be vulnerable that allows us to see it. When I realised this, I cried to let go of all the energy it took to always keep myself and my emotions together. Facing our worst fears has its own freedom. So this incredible insight made me realise why it was so important to create gentle platforms for women who withdraw, to do this for themselves as they experience themselves removed from their own power. It is true that no one can take our power from us, we have given it away at some point. If we give it away, we can also ask for it back. Awareness starts there, but awareness alone is not enough.

The next step is choosing to engage, which requires feeling a gentleness of safety and compassion from those involved. We need an environment to support us to feel safe within ourselves.

Nurturing pain

Nurturing ourselves is not just taking care of ourselves physically and feeling child-like emotions again. The baggage women hold onto needs to go. Old emotions keep us from the freedom to love someone else without reservation. Some women prefer to feel entitled because of old emotions that need to be taken care of instead, and would rather be abused than leave their husbands. Exchanging what she has to offer for safety, in mind and body, is not love. When the baggage goes, her lust for life returns and she can do anything, one step at a time. Women are designed to be connected to their inner selves enough to catch the fleeting thought that says: "Go read that book or light this candle."

To nurture themselves, women need to learn to trust their intuition to guide them again.

Nurturing does not mean being in control

Don't confuse the ability to nurture yourself with the expectation that your mind controls every moment. Nor does it know beforehand what will have to happen. When you do need to know something – you will. Trust that, and believe that everything you need to have is already available. Therein is a big truth, because every woman wants to trust in a man. But how can she trust you when she cannot trust herself yet?

Unless we truly understand the power of being vulnerable again, we miss out on the benefits of the feminine spirit – of being open to receive, to laugh and to love without fear. Vulnerability says gift me, but always remember she too is able to gift herself with nurturing. If however, you wish to gift your partner she will accept without expectation as you see her beautiful – a soul mirror.

Tips for nurturing her

- ☯ Help her to help herself.
- ☯ Teach her to be open to receiving by repeating the experiences of giving.
- ☯ Notice at what stage she is expecting you to give to her and stop giving.
- ☯ She is now invited to give to herself, because she will recognise what it feels like to receive in this way.
- ☯ If she cannot receive what you give, encourage her to give herself permission to receive.
- ☯ If needed, do this for yourself without guilt, and notice her reflections as you just hold space for her.
- ☯ Smile when she blames you for being selfish, which is really her own projection of rejecting nurturing, which turns her inwards. Reacting to her words might add fuel to the fire and keep her from her inner journey.
- ☯ Invite her to accept what she rejects in her own mother more and more.
- ☯ Ask her questions about who fulfils her needs, and what her expectations are. Encourage her with practical steps to fulfil her own needs.
- ☯ More than anything, let your conversations become a safe space for her to be emotionally vulnerable and express her real needs.
- ☯ Appreciate her honesty and courage to open herself when she expresses her feelings about herself. Notice where you can give her expressions value.
- ☯ Help her to identify her feelings of rejection as self-judgement, and let her know that no one will judge her if she doesn't judge herself.
- ☯ Ask her if she notices any patterns in the areas of her life or events over time, when she expresses them. In the words she uses, she will reveal the core imprints that drive her behaviour.

- If her emotions are traumatic and irrational, allow her to make the decision about being safe enough to be alone with her feelings, until she chooses to do this by herself. If you don't feel that you can hold the space for her to experience her emotions, ask her very gently to speak to someone she trusts who can hold the space for her in a safe environment. Never push her.
- Encourage her to trust her intuition to guide her without controlling it.

Chapter 21

Time exists for you

Space to accommodate your creation

You are no victim of circumstance

When will you realise that you are your soul's creation?

I am you

– Experience Flow

Learning Consciously Through Conflict

Observing conflict in conscious relationships allows us to become aware of how much we experience each other as separate from ourselves, instead of reflections of each other. Conflict gives us the opportunity to experience wholeness because we can use it as a tool in our relationship to apply our new-found values. We already know that we will attract the imprint of ourselves that we rejected naturally. Therefore conflict in conscious relationships is natural. What we can do is choose how we experience those parts of ourselves that we still need to accept.

The pain of rejecting parts of ourselves brings up anger that hides the pain. Often during times of conflict we speak from pain through anger. As your partner experiences your projected anger, she will close the openness. As your door into her closes, the growth in the relationship is also stunted.

Choosing to engage with the conflicting issue can break down the relationship.

Conflict is safe within boundaries

All relationships, of a personal or professional nature, are built on trust. As we learn to trust each other we can create a safe boundary in which to experience apparent differences. We're not each other's enemies, although at times it might feel like that. That idea or belief that we hold onto so much is an attachment that separates us from each other if we don't agree on it. Do we now give up who we are and what we stand for or allow the conflict to build a wall between us? How do we consciously create safe borders within which to communicate? What happens when the emotional build-up of our stuff gets so intense that we cannot hear each other?

There are many wonderful conflict resolutions available like the *Imago dialogue* and *Time to think*. But what I will discuss here are the rules of engagement in conscious relationships, in order to demonstrate that natural conflict can help us to develop deeper trust in one another.

Holes in our boundaries will allow things to attach. Conflict is one way in which to make conscious what comes up for healing. When we aren't so eager to defend the ideas we're holding onto, there is no need for conflict. Every conflict is an opportunity to heal something inside us. If and when we can approach those dreaded moments like this, they change our experience and perspective of conflict. This understanding comes with some new thought-provoking values, which are worth considering as rules of engagement, if they can be respected by both partners.

I find two techniques very useful. Start each sentence in the first person "I..." or instead of making a statement to offer an opinion, to ask a question that starts with ***"Can I assume that...?"***

To the person receiving the information, what was previously experienced as a projection is heard as a question in an authentic experience, attributed to the one speaking, instead of you. This is a

lot less confrontational and allows the listener to hear a lot more before they shut down emotionally because they feel attacked. With every question the input of the listener is required to create a platform of opinions on which conclusions can be drawn in an *overlapped map,* as opposed to just offering an individual opinion from a personal map. It also helps a lot with focussed conversations that both the listener and communicator can follow. Examples are:
- "You hurt me" is replaced with *"I got hurt when you touched me"*
- "Did you really have to do that?" is replaced with *"Can I assume that you did that because you had to understand what was happening?"*

The changes are subtle, but less confrontational, and say the same thing with a more constructive informational slant.

Conflict rules of engagement for respect, trust and equality
- Conscious relationships require honest expression.
- Complete honesty accelerates personal growth and self-knowledge.
- The best defence is offence – when one partner challenges a belief, we can un-believe or become aware of what in us needs to believe that. Instead of buying into conditioned beliefs, we can try to understand what motivated it and what need in us was served by believing that.
- Partners provide us with the most vulnerable reflection of ourselves and mirror where we can experience the safest place within which to express our deepest needs, outside of ourselves.
- Struggling with conflict reflects our internal conflict outside of ourselves.
- Our partners help us to experience reflections of ourselves, in order to accelerate personal growth.

- ❧ Conflict allows the release of tension, which creates energy to connect deeply with another and, by default, connect with ourselves.
- ❧ Unexpressed ambiguity in the field creates conflict, and we need to find words to convey this gently. Any unexpressed ambiguity will play out in drama. Addressing it directly brings it into the open.
- ❧ Engaging with conflict in relationships reflects our inner conflict with the self, and how we attempt to heal it. This is what will take us to the next level of growth.
- ❧ Conflict resolutions teach us to allow compassionate listening, which is an essential life skill for healing.
- ❧ What we cannot express clearly to our partners, we project onto them. What we cannot own as our stuff, we blame our partners for. Everything we don't think is mine or ours, is exactly what still hides from us.
- ❧ Conflict dissipates naturally without tension when it's served its purpose. Any emotionally loaded conflict reflects that we are probably projecting onto our partner. If the conflict experienced is painful, the pain tells us that we have stuff to heal and this conflict helps us to become whole.

Conflict is a way of communicating to grow

Remember that what you resist persists. So the conflict you avoid will find you, wherever you hide. Find your personal tools for dealing with it and let conflict serve you well. The miracle cure is surrender. When and if you can find it in your heart to express your emotions, own what is yours and forgive yourself.

Learning through conflict is recognising that disagreement doesn't resonate with the love that accepts each other. But allowing our partner's *free will* keeps us in a place of love rather than succumbing to separating who is right from who is wrong. Keep an inclusive attitude and be self-sovereign in your approach to keeping judgement at bay. Be present during your partner's internal struggle and notice how it brings up your own stuff for integration.

Remember: Rather vote for the relationship with your heart than focus on who is right or wrong.

Use this opportunity as a reflection to yourself, as a mirror, to notice parts of you that you may have rejected.

Allow yourself to be healed. Accept that the part that you resist has a role to play in the right situation and serves your highest potential.

Start by listening to your partner's view (or what created the conflict), and then tolerate the thought, assuming he or she is right. What might the implication of that be? What does that say about you? What if you could accept that it may be true? Could you even appreciate that point of view because you understand the underlying intention?

Internal resistance expresses outward as conflict

Resistance is the process that shows us where we can love ourselves more. In truth, resistance comes from rejected parts of ourselves that need a purpose to exist inside us. When we recognise the message, it starts to sabotage our efforts from the background. How many more ways can we find out who we are? And if this is not the highest and best part of us, does it not also deserve our love? Everything we suppress will control our actions from the background. And not all emotional baggage has memories to explain its existence in a logical way. A fully integrated partner is one who knows who he or she is and is willing to get to know more about themselves. This partner will be prepared to listen compassionately to what emotions need to express for healing during conflict. Become a conflict junkie. Welcome conflict and notice how it can create havoc, just because hidden needs are allowed to be there.

Learn to see your partner as an extension of yourself. Treat all conflict in the same way you would have discussed the issue with God himself.

Be easy on yourself – unpack the facts from the emotion
Don't allow emotions to take over and control what is happening. Instead, notice how they are attached to limiting beliefs and learn to contain them within safe boundaries. Allow emotions to teach you what you don't know and interpret them as messages for correction in your quiet time.

Sometimes there is no logical answer when we separate the facts from the emotions and all we can do is sit with it. In my experience, the answers do come eventually when I just observe with compassion and without judging. When the insights do come, notice in how many areas of your life you can apply the learning.

There is no better way to learn from conflict than with the partner we have chosen for life, because he or she reflects, more than anyone, how we see ourselves, even when we cannot yet understand the value of the lesson. For me, this sharing is what makes me want to be in a conscious relationship, rather than just being with someone who meets my needs.

The irony is that this is easier for you to do, as her partner, than it is for her. But then you already know this. You can teach her this if you choose to stand back from your ego's need to be right. She will be with her emotion and still separate the emotions from the facts if she doesn't have to justify her intuitive side's existence. Maybe if we stop pushing, needing to prove a point through some internal strategy to manipulate the situation, we'll realise which thought is the most important to focus on now. This is what frees us from the emotional overload.

If you aren't called *always right* and she doesn't have to tolerate *being wrong* then your communication through conflict has the potential to deepen your intimacy by breaking down the walls between you, instead of conflict building the walls higher. Allow her to find her own solution by just being there for her, but be present mentally, physically and emotionally.

Conflict tips

- Cultivate an approach to accept conflict as necessary for growth.
- Accept conflict as an opportunity to accept more of the self you reject.
- Notice that emotions indicate your own reflection.
- Wait until it is safe to talk without confronting each other.
- Be willing to see your partner's perspective on the matter.
- Become soft in yourself before you engage in conversation.
- Create safe boundaries for conflict and respect your partner's needs.
- Discuss what worked about the conversations after you have them, or practice with *Imago* and *Time to think* techniques if you cannot find your own way.
- Be gentle but honest.
- Find time to work on yourself as you discover your stuff.
- Own your participation in what created the conflict.
- The ratio for balance is one negative for every five positives. Appreciate your partner with each conflict when it is resolved.
- Resolved issues will leave you feeling closer than before.
- Separate emotions from facts.

Chapter 22

֍ Creation out of the chaos

Structure out of abyss

Riding the waves of the ocean

Or staying afloat waiting, choosing not to

No right or wrong

Just expressing who we are in the moment

Embody the meaning of life

Like the wizard and sorceress of old ֍

– Alchemy Signature

Developing Feminine Leadership Skills

I used to wonder why husbands phoned me to coach their wives who wished to re-enter the workspace, instead of the women themselves. I realised that men could see their partner's value more clearly than women could or would admit to themselves. Apparently women are the ones who fail to realise what a valuable role they play in society as a whole, at home and potentially in the world of work.

What is feminine leadership?
Many women in leadership roles act like men because research still shows that people prefer a deeper voice. But there is a bigger case for feminine leadership than ever before, as women bring balance into the business world. The best business case for feminine leadership today is that women instil trust. Feminine leaders flow harmoniously and easily, without the painful push that often accompanies the masculine drive and competitive nature. Pressure and non-performance in business ask for the next level of leadership, which comes with collaboration and inner wisdom that recognises personal integrity, listening with heart and passion. What feminine leadership is not, is overpowering the sacred

masculine leadership because it is seen as better. Feminine leadership is that of equality and has a healthy, integrated leadership style rather than an over-developed masculine style. It can call on the benefits of both gender strengths in appropriate situations, finding a sweet spot for maximum, healthy, sustainable output. Feminine leaders show up in the boardroom as women, playing that role with many men and with many women, and using gender leadership skills to bring balance.

A feminine leader takes time to tap into her inner wisdom and work on her relationship with herself, nurturing herself and using reflections of self in her different relationships. She is emotionally free of the need for approval and leads authentically, bringing her contribution into the world with confidence to make the biggest difference she can. She doesn't ask permission to take the lead and express her highest values. She never abandons herself for any reason, but acts from a place of passion.

Assist her to recognise her natural skills
The truth is that women are scared of their own power. They are also not always equipped to recognise what is so natural and inherent to them, and seem to wait for someone else to recognise it first. Even when she leads, it is gently with wisdom and insight. It is done so gracefully it looks like she's doing nothing – she listens more than she speaks and develops deep empathy skills that develop those around her in a supportive way.

Encourage her emotional intelligence
Unlike a man, she doesn't lead predominantly with intellectual intelligence, but with emotional intelligence. She accesses her intuition and acts in a way that considers all the parties involved, to encourage loyalty and ownership in business. She often doesn't even recognise herself as a leader, operating under the radar to create harmony and peace.

Women increase human capital and shift perspectives

She naturally understands other people and what they need. Her nurturing ability assists other people and brings balance into the work space. She develops others rather than focussing only on herself, which they return with loyalty and trust. She gives people feedback in ways that build their image of themselves, and if she has to criticise, she does it in the gentlest possible manner. She challenges people to live up to their potential by believing in them and tasking them accordingly. She has a special ability to see things from another's perspective and to ask questions when someone is stuck in a negative frame of mind.

Feminine energy is like glue for diversity and potential conflict

She has a deep respect for people and is sensitive to diverse worldviews when people are not like her. She spots social networks and reads political currents in organisations. She influences with her thoughts, and indirectly uses complicated strategies to build consensus and support. She can listen through an entire boardroom meeting when men are all talking at the same time, and when she speaks she will say the one thing everyone else failed to hear, closing the discussion in finality. What would have distracted the masculine focus, the feminine will include in her decision-making process as supporting information. She will support her decisions with insightful observations that he may find irrelevant.

Women make great managers

In communication, she reads the emotional and body cues and creates rapport with others. She is willing to address difficult issues in a discussion style and welcomes the sharing of information while she listens. She is receptive to good and bad news. She inspires people with her shared vision. When she can assist, she will step forward. She holds people accountable and leads by example, rather than using words to instruct leadership.

Her feminine leadership skills will be her advantage

The most important role a man can play in his partner's development is helping her to recognise her leadership skills. The workplace is performance-driven to the extent that the average CEO has a life cycle of 18 months, according to research in the United States. And many high-level managers prefer a sabbatical between contracts. If a person can incorporate personal development into their lifestyle in a way that encourages them to observe their own thoughts and feelings, the mind will self-correct, heal and balance.

Too much "go-go" energy without breakaway time has cultivated a different type of leader in business today, one who needs regular sabbaticals to recharge. Feminine leaders change that with their ability to empathise in a performance-driven environment, which prevents what have become accepted yet expensive breakaways.

Assist her to understand how tangible her value is

When feminine leadership balances the working environment with listening and receptive energy, the quality of experience in organisations is richer and more fulfilling. Feminine leadership is in its infancy as women are only now entering an equal place from which to lead in principle, but this is not yet reflected in statistics. The number of women leading in a masculine style is not doing business any favours.

Women still need to find their own ways to express their leadership in a way that will contend with powerful leaders. Many are still in their own practices, where they don't have to play the competitive game, or learn how to integrate their inner masculine and feminine. By encouraging your partner to be herself and to see the role that she can play in society, you'll give her the confidence she needs to express herself in different ways.

Feminine leadership summary

Men often value women more than they value themselves. Feminine leadership is challenging the perception that women develop a masculine skill as business discovers the value of collaboration, wisdom and integrity for human capital. This new leadership style harnesses the powerful balance towards equality that makes working hours meaningful and motivates untapped potential. Her management skills develop people and she supports diversity with inclusion. Business needs more women to lead under the radar, and by example, as they inspire and perform through accountability.

Chapter 23

My chest is moving up and down

My breath is deep and full

Conscious in this moment

My eyes perceive the colour of love

My hands feel the texture of depth

And sounds of silence fill my ears

Soft pale skin luxuriously smooth

In my mind's eye

Melting into the energy that surrounds

– Pure and Sensual

What Happened To Intimacy And Sensual Expression?

The deepest desire she has is to experience connection and intimacy. As her appointed and most vulnerable reflection of herself, she craves to see herself in you as she did when you were in love. This was when she felt the most beautiful. So what happened to all that? Why is she not intimately close to you and experiencing her body in the sensual, wonderful way that made you fall in love with her?

The essence of the feminine provides the flow in the relationship and the masculine creates the structure for her to flow. They exist together to co-create a river. You build the banks of the river and she is the water. What makes contained water a river is that it flows on a path of its own accord. The relationship is then represented by the river, which is different to the water and the banks that contain it.

What is intimacy?
Intimacy is the way the roles in the relationship flow, which gives an experience of closeness where she can be her soft self without having to close up. It is a wonderful place with no walls between

two people, where the relationship reflects openness and transparency with the self. There is nothing she will not do and no conditions of exchange. No one needs forgiving and everything is allowed. Life is experienced through the senses with such clarity of vision and inner peace. She is completely herself and wholeheartedly accepts whatever she wishes to contribute. What the relationship reflects is a wonderful, safe place where her inner masculine and inner feminine are married and flow together.

There are some factors to keep in mind, which influence the levels of intimacy we are able to experience in the relationship.

Rigid, defined roles kill our freedom
When we're ready for a relationship, we define our own roles based on what we believe we can bring to the flow and structures of the river. When we're not ready for the responsibility of relationships, we find ourselves lacking in our understanding of the original reason for roles. When we don't know why the roles are there and just accept them during the relationship's romantic stages, we become inflexible.

If we feel that we had little choice but to accept the roles, at times when our circumstance left us no other option, we develop resistance and this breaks down intimacy. Even if we verbally agree to do something, it doesn't mean we're ready to take on that responsibility. Anything that feels like it curbs our freedom makes us feel as if we have abandoned a part of ourselves.

Accepting responsibilities because we are ready for them allows us the transparency that is needed between two intimate partners who are ready to open up, to discover more of themselves through discovery and sharing on all levels, including the senses of taste, smell and touch.

By questioning our roles before we accept them, we find the original purpose of the responsibility. It changes everything when we act within our own integrity and are true to who we are. This not only leads to freedom but also to an experience of gender equality inside a relationship, where two people work together responsibly to fulfil their soul contracts.

How can we bring intimacy back into gender roles?
If the structured roles that we end up with are what break down our ability to be intimate with each other, it seems obvious that we need to find a way to restore intimacy by closing the gap that was created in the first place. We do this by looking at ways to grow closer to each other's internal realities. We look naturally towards communication and possibly how to resolve conflict. I would like to suggest that for intimacy we look even deeper than that: that we look at our common and different values, as well as our ability to develop what we now know as our inner feminine and masculine.

Seeking common values
The overlap between two individual's values is where we acknowledge what is the same for both of us. Growth comes in the relationship as we communicate through speaking the same value-language. Just like we fell in love initially with the reflection of ourselves rather than really seeing the other person, this type of communication breaks down walls and shows us the foundation on which our relationship is built, and whether it is solid or fragile. Similarly, communicating conflict shows us where we still have different values or ideas. The space to hold diversity and inclusion in relationships comes from our level of consciousness, despite our unique expressions of self. I was once told that I'm a powerful being despite my positive or negative emotional state. And the truth is we are all like that, we are bigger than the emotions we feel.

Trust your partner, responsibly, where your values don't overlap
Where our values no longer overlap determines the extent of our necessary growth, and where the journey of trust begins through

our personal masculine and feminine developmental stages. As we move between the sexual essences of two polarised sides, our baggage will show up and provide opportunities to heal. Our ability to trust or not to trust someone else depends on how much we need to learn to trust ourselves.

Our self-worth is based on the thoughts we have of who we think we are, extended into the values we apply to ourselves based on our importance compared to someone else. Trust infers that we are all equal. The inner masculine and feminine are what invite us to draw on these aspects of self to be recognised inside ourselves and attract us to each other. The inner masculine and feminine also show us how much work we need to do to experience intimacy and a sensual engagement with life and each other, as we resist each other. This creates sexual tension.

In principal, moving through these value sets, the feminine flows into the masculine structures. If we look at how they work together as the water flows, we can learn to see what happened to our sensuality and intimacy in the feminine and masculine over time.

History of structure and flow development, becoming one

Before we can discuss development, allow me to remind you about the basic essence of the container and the water. Here a container would be what we have previously referred to as the glass that holds the water. The glass then represents the basic male essence and the water the basic female essence. The male and female energies are separate and individual and there is no *development* when they are merely perceived as a half-full or half-empty glass of water. Only when water moves can this be depicted as development because now the male and female aspects interact. On its own, male energy creates structure and form, like the glass that gives the water shape. On its own, female energy is flexible and fills the shape of any container. Whether the glass is half full or half empty is an illusion – our focus creates our perception. But when there is movement the river symbolises the introduction of a new level of consciousness – the separate male and female as a *relationship*, which is dynamic and keeps changing.

At first, clear gender roles define the female flow and the male banks to create natural and harmonious small rivers through the lands.

Male-dominated systems control and force the female flow of water. Naturally, as the female's flow is restricted in its movement, the back and forth interplay of water overflows the structures to return the balance of nature. Now the female dominates as it creates and directs the waterways, while the man stays in control of the river banks, even when the system isn't working as it should be.

During the next stage, men become more involved with the flow of the water and the females become more involved in building the structures for the river, based on individual purposes (not necessarily shared). What this symbolises in practice is that males became more sensitive and the females become performance-driven and focussed. It is clear that in the development of the male and female archetypes, the original roles are now reversing.

Finally, both the male and female archetypes realise that it makes no sense to be both the structure and the flow simultaneously. Everyone returns to the original roles of structure and flow, except that now they are more appreciative and understanding of the opposite role's responsibilities and gifts. As equal partners, male and female co-create, and can take on the opposite role's responsibility when needed. This is how, through a maturity process, a codependent relationship is avoided and instead, when the masculine gifts the feminine, it's appreciated and not expected.

Understanding the dynamic of polarity to create growth
For people in general, it is preferable to have partners with mostly overlapping values. They make best friends and the relationship is

nurturing. They refer loosely to having a soul mate who understands them well. This is not necessarily what a growth relationship is like where the opposite partners invite growth to heal.

What becomes clear is that what started out, in the most extreme polarities of opposite male and female roles, is also what originally created sexual tension.

It is this sexual tension that feels like the original, irresistible chemistry, which becomes the basis for intimate relationship where we experience sensuality and intimacy with each other.

As this tension from the polarity that attracts male and female begs to be connected, they also define and redefine their roles and play them out through the development of a relationship and individual identities. When the male and females roles overlap, the sexual tension is reduced in intensity until, at the end of the process, we achieve the same levels of sexual polarity again. Now we have depth and understanding for each other's gender essence and integrate more of our own inner masculine and feminine.

Blame signifies lack of responsibility for our role participation

At some point the male collective, quick to point out women's lack of focus to be who she wants to be, will own its part in the development of his story.

When you don't take responsibility, it's directly related to your lack of understanding about role responsibilities, and the same goes for women. When she doesn't feel beautiful anymore, she lets herself go and displays her stand on accepting her role in the collective. Some women will eat to substitute the attention they seek and get attention even if it's negative. Other women eat to fill the emptiness in their souls, because their male counterparts don't know how to keep them open anymore and don't take responsibility for their masculine roles, which leaves her poorly supported to turn her development inwards. She blames him for all her trouble. As he moves his gaze away from her and towards his vocation, an escape to deal with his inner resistances in the relationship, it's wise for her to be encouraged to learn the skills of self-nurturing and not to rely on him when she feels unsafe. Later she cannot blame him for hurting her because she learns to keep herself safe and fulfil her own needs. If she doesn't know who she is and depends on him for feedback about her beauty, she will eat more to fill that soul need, and be even needier for his approval than before.

Sensuality is natural for a woman who feels beautiful

When unnoticed, women appear as the opposite of sensual, especially when they lack the ability to notice themselves. The Marilyn Monroe story revealed a great number of insights about the sexually desired woman. Watching the portrayal in the latest movie about her, I was surprised at how insecure Marilyn was compared to my perception of her. She needed constant affirmation of her value, by both her agent and the men she attracted into her personal space. Marilyn was all about attention and she showed the camera her vulnerability, magnetising men to project their masculinity onto her. Marilyn was depicted in the movie of her life as a needy woman. To perform, she needed to feel beautiful all the time. If she couldn't connect with that part of herself, she had no confidence to act in front of the camera. During such times she was tranquilised to move beyond her self-consciousness in order to perform on stage. In the end, you wonder if being a desired woman in the eyes of the world was worth her constant insecurity and lack of self-nurturing. Her death was described by some as someone who wanted to escape from the constant public gaze, in need of one private moment. I wonder if Marilyn could ever decide for herself whether she was beautiful. She appeared to rely on everyone else to tell her, and if she wasn't convinced of it, she was sedated to keep her moods at bay. Of course, it doesn't have to turn out like this for sensual women. A sensual woman is someone in touch with her senses and body; she is grounded. This woman brings a man out of his head and into his body by engaging his heart.

A woman who conquers her insecurity and who is able to be open despite her past pain is very much an authentic, sensual being.

Sexual polarity is influenced by values evolving through consciousness. Initially, the media creates expectations of what sexuality is. Then our mental maps are matured through life's experiences. We experience the difference between the masculine and the feminine energy of the mind, and once we accept them individually, we integrate both. It is the polarity that creates this sexual attraction. The imprint of what we don't think we are is exactly what attracts us to each other. In the same way, it becomes the obstacle we eventually embrace in order to integrate and become whole beings.

We also know that intimacy is not necessarily linked to sexual activity, as demonstrated by the animal world, but it makes experiencing sensuality a holistic and full experience. The more intimate we are able to be, the deeper our experience of life and the more sensual we appear to the world as it too can feel our essence. Masculine and feminine energies require each other to balance the relationship. It is this different gender expression of humanity that draws each other close, and the very opposite polarity creates the physical connection we refer to as a sexual experience on a primal level. The stronger the individual male or female identity, the more they bring out the opposite in each other. When an authentic male or female essence is not present, we are cut off from our natural desires, our love of life and our sexuality. The more we are able to be just who we are as male or female, the more we accept life with its imperfections, and our reflections of self in our partners.

We can be cut off from our own consciousness by unconscious behaviour, which keeps us cut off from our life connection when we are not authentic. Our loss of connection to our own soul undermines our ability to be sensual.

Polarity sets the stage for intimacy

With no polarity there is little sexual attraction. Stated differently, two people who are too much alike and who don't experience the masculine and feminine energy polarity will have diminished sexual desire. The smaller the gap between them, the smaller the push-pull movement of contraction and expansion needed for creation. Expressing masculine or feminine energy can be suppressed inside males and females because they overdevelop an opposite inner masculine or feminine, which kills our natural desire. As parents, we meet our children's requests with a constant no. Eventually our kids' natural curiosity is overridden by cultural rules and parents' expectations of behaviour. This disconnects children from their own desire, as they try to please us. We unconsciously instil fear and an unnatural need to please others in our children. Telling kids what they need also disconnects them from connecting easily with their own souls, and inhibits their ability to live sensually.

Comfort food will never satisfy our conditioned, distorted physical needs and beliefs. Our distortions show up as cravings for food because our parents didn't nurture us. Accordingly, we don't know how to nurture ourselves. Alcohol brings no spirit, and sex brings no union. Our craving for intimacy is a soul calling to feed our soul's connection to our own inner source in life, through sharing with our partner. Polarity in partnerships evolves us by meeting our soul desires.

You are the power of her beauty

Initially, females hope that they'll feel beautiful from their experience of what you share with them about their beauty. Marilyn Monroe relied completely on what people told her about her appearance before she could act in front of a camera. Depending on an external reference for recognising who we are as women, is not sustainable. The antidote is developing the ability to self-nurture and a sincere understanding of our needs. Released from the approval of others and learning a new internal feedback system she can trust, based on her relationship with herself, she develops her own self-esteem and reveals her inner beauty. No pursuit of beauty through a salon or spa, surgery or exercise will substitute for the experience of being appreciated enough to know forever that she is beautiful. Without knowing how the feminine feels the love that trusts life, she will live in fear of living. Women even create the illusion of security by watching predictable soap operas, or surrounding themselves with many possessions and beautiful items to believe they are loved. Until she realises that there must be another way, she won't look deeper than skin deep for inner beauty. She'll play the game that exchanges her contribution for finding meaning and purpose, rather than give for the joy of it.

Women have a way to use sensual expression with impure intentions. If, as young women we didn't quite connect with what we offer our communities and the world in terms of what is uniquely ours, we become dependent on those who appreciate our beauty to tell us what our purpose in life is.

This makes us vulnerable to those we give our power to as women and, in turn, we are prepared to exchange our sexual wares for what we think we want. The stage is set for a game that plays out. When we seem vulnerable, it drives the unconscious primal male urge to take advantage of our feminine vulnerability. The opposite is also true; when the feminine understands her value and purpose she cannot be taken advantage of and doesn't attract relationships in which she feels used.

At this stage with this imprint, the female will use what she has to get what she wants and considers this a fair exchange, not knowing that at some point her soul will beckon her to see her own beauty. Sometimes when she is desperate, she will prostitute her soul because she cannot access a new and different mental map to get what she really wants.

Marilyn was a beautiful woman who was very needy because she couldn't see her own beauty and needed other people to reflect it back to her constantly. She understood how to use her gifts to get what she wanted. No man could satisfy her, because the way she went about seducing men attracted men who focussed on her outer need. External needs might not be in sync with the inner intimacy that her soul craves. To link outer need with intimate connection, you require purity of intention through your actions, and that starts with the ability to know and express your soul need to a partner.

If Marilyn was able to fill her own needs through self-nurturing, she might have gained the respect she desired from those who surrounded her. She would still appreciate the male gaze, but would not depend on it as her life force.

Eventually, through the maturity of the male and female roles, the male does appreciate the beauty of a woman, and she sees and knows her own beauty. What could allow her to live her beauty more sensually in everything she does than that?

Give her power back to enhance intimacy
There is something you can do to encourage her to access her own beauty without her giving her power to you. There are some questions to explore and each one will bring her closer to the way

she sees herself, to reframe her story as she has been telling it to herself until now.

Know that her saying it out loud to you, the most important person in her life who experiences her vulnerability, allows her to hear her version of her story too. By saying it out aloud, she claims it as her truth. If you take time to listen for understanding, this acknowledges her just as she is. There is no one more important than you to whom she can reveal her beauty as she discovers it. At this point, less feedback has more value to her. It allows an experience to form her own belief in herself without depending on anyone.

Ask her what her contribution is
Every woman has a story of how she learned about her womanhood. Her first experience and how her womanhood was celebrated are definitive in her value of herself as a woman, by overcoming the mystery of not bleeding to death. When her story is something that she tells with pride, she will know who she is and may sense what she is here to contribute to society.

Recently I read a local article where feedback was asked from the readers about how a young girl's first menses could be celebrated. The answers were more about how shameful it was to even discuss the topic without any readers acknowledging the value of the initiation itself. Reading this, I realised how far removed we are as women from connecting with our natural gifts as nurturers of society.

Often women who have painful periods, have stories related to their lack of understanding of the depth of the spiritual lessons that later determine their ability to fill their intense soul desire to connect intimately with a partner. To be a sensual creature with soft curves, accepting of ourselves, we need to embrace what it means to us to be a woman. If there is any way in which you can assist your partner to experience her story as a hero's journey, her inner beauty will shine through, as if it's the most natural thing in the world and without her even knowing she is being perceived as radiant.

What does she really want from sharing with a partner she can trust?

Are you afraid she might ask for something that you aren't able to provide? Just ease into the question. What she is asking you is really a soul question directed at herself. Her soul will ask her to create a sacred projection of the ideal partner (you), but the reverse is actually what we are asking here: What does that ideal man, with the pure heart whom she shares with openly and intimately, want in a partner? Is this her or is she left wanting? What is it about this invisible woman that her own soul is calling out for? Is it possible she is this person in hiding? Sharing requires mirroring, validating and empathy.

What have people said about her in the past that touched her, true or not?

She will remember how people made her feel rather than the facts about what happened. The feelings she remembers are reflections of what she can own or disown about herself, and may indicate unhealed pain that is still present. What she chooses to express about the feelings she remembers indicates what the unconscious is ready to reveal, as she might now be ready to heal it by accepting it as truth. Your partner may be that good person or the one who always does the right thing because of her upbringing. Maybe her parents' rules asked her to reject her own feelings and now they come up through her emotions when other people make comments about her. At some point, she had to accept her parents' rules over her own emotions, but now she can own her own feelings and still be reasonable enough to act appropriately. Maybe accepting these parts of herself will allow her to be who she is more fully. And you can be the one who listens to her new story, understands it and supports her in her growth. Could we then experience ourselves just for who we are, instead of feeling like we have to prove something to society?

Sensuality disappears when we stop exploring curiously and fall into the trap of playing out roles. We start to see ourselves through our partner's eyes and believe that that is all we can be.

If you see her as beautiful, tell her. If you want her sensuality to return to you, allow her to experience your transparency and come close to you without expecting anything from her. See her for who she is rather than what you want from her. Is this person in hiding?

Vulnerability is powerful when it is authentic

The difference between being a needy, wounded woman and a powerful, authentic beauty lies in her willingness to nurture herself. Not every willing woman has the resources, but what she does have is an open heart. Pain that closes hearts is only the faces of ourselves that we rejected on our journey and now refuse to accept. As long as we fight it, it will let us see the imprint of rejecting what we are. When our hearts are open, even while we feel pain, allows us to be vulnerable as a reminder of what the pain was like, having recall of experiences. When we are strong enough to keep our hearts open while this happens, the magic happens and we take our power back. We realise that to feel is OK, and if we allow this, we know that we can handle it too. No one else has the power to hurt us. We accept this and have the ability to make new meanings that will serve us in the future. These are the moments when the pain we tried so hard to avoid disappears ... and during these moments, we accept the truth about ourselves.

Encourage her to express her value

Every woman's deepest desire is to connect intimately with her partner and to see herself as desirable and beautiful through his complete acceptance of her. The relationship provides the platform for her to experience herself as fully feminine with a close-up reflection in a safe space to be vulnerable. The closeness of being intimate is limited when gender role expectations are rigid. Accepting responsibilities without understanding the needs they serve doesn't meet our need to be who we are in the relationship. With more unmet expectations come more walls that prevent the openness required for intimacy. Respect for each other's expressed needs creates equality that nurtures intimacy. Meeting our own core needs also allows us to appreciate our partner's value. Seeing our values in our partner brings reflections that acknowledge how much of ourselves is in our partner and what can be closer than that?

With each projection where we can acknowledge our participation, even if it's painful, we invite compassion into the sacred space between two people. Intimacy supports us to trust ourselves when we feel insecure. The closer we become, the safer it feels to relive vulnerabilities and make new constructive meanings that support every experience, sense of belonging and self-esteem. The dance of masculine and feminine polarity brings the necessary tension to experience attraction to our own reflection, which we need to be complete human beings.

The very opposite qualities, which initially attract and which we later resist, are what bring two people together. The satisfaction of intimacy that leaves two lovers to go their separate ways brings them together again, like the momentum of a stretched rubber band when it is pulled too far apart in two separate directions.

Women experience life sensually when they feel appreciated and accepted. Everything looks more beautiful and intense. The more radiant she looks, the more she commands the gaze of men. Her innocence brings purity. On the contrary, needy women drive the very intimacy they crave from their partners away. The more we know and accept ourselves, the more we are able to experience another person without the resistance of walls in between. Conditioning and pain shut us down from experiencing intimacy. Women who believe they are beautiful do so because men told them so. Give her her power back so she can know her inner beauty. The more she feels secure in herself, the more open she feels, which allows her inhibitions to disappear and she becomes more curious. Encourage her to express her value as she discovers herself, and notice the quality of your intimacy change. Trust and safe boundaries bring the right conditions for a firm intimate foundation where both your needs for sharing can be met. Grow your intimacy with the curiosity that comes with freedom, to express yourselves in new ways. Witness any painful moments when they show up as moments of grace when you can accept more of yourselves.

Chapter 24

☙ Once upon a time, a long time ago, there was a woman who became a girl. She was a golden girl who shone brightly as she lived a life of discovery in the world of love. Then one day she met a master who taught her to experience what was not love. She cried and cried for all she knew was love. What to make of this strange lesson?

A little bird sat on a tree close to her and told her the secret of existence. Nothing that you see is real; all that matters is what you choose to feel. Soon she forgot and played with the butterflies that touched her with their magical freedom. And in a moment of passionate skipping, out of the corner of her eye, she noticed the master looking into her soul. And then she felt it again… a completeness that faded the seeming reality into pure love.

For the lesson was that all is love. When love is itself in its purity it cannot experience itself. But when the little girl saw her reflection in the master, the butterfly, and everything else, she remembered who she really was… ❧

– The Golden Girl

Did You See Me Naked?

Life sets the stage to teach women about real beauty through accepting their nakedness. Only if we're willing to take off the masks, personality, make-up and everything we cover natural beauty with, can we truly transform as we accept our born nature. At the age of three we already have the conditioned imprint as girls to become objects to be viewed. Little boys are praised when they can manipulate their environments to show strength. Then we learn to unlearn it all beyond roles as men and women. We learn to see ourselves without the clothes and what our conditioning brings. In work, we focus on performance despite the gender stereotype and put the right person in the position. In relationships, the male can stay at home if the woman wants to exercise her choice to focus on a career. We learn that despite our grooming, we choose our roles. And inside us the same is happening as we evolve spiritually and we meet our inner masculine and feminine.

Give the feminine a real voice

My name is Adelé, and it means both "to be humble" and "from the aristocracy", depending on how you pronounce it. I am a paradox. That is how we recognise truth. A coin has two sides. Women are both dark and light, and when we are naked we claim both the clothes that highlight our strengths and the vulnerability that leaves us cold. To find my voice, I accept all of me and as I do, the light shines on my shadow and that heals me. The triggers that activate our transformation encourage us to feel and grow more than just thinking allows us to grow. As we struggle to find the words and language to express what is going on, we are dealing with the birthing of a new voice. How we negotiate with our relationship with ourselves, will determine how our masculine is invited to join us.

Making way for the emerging feminine

Transitioning women are mirrors of the soul for all who choose to look at them, especially their partners. How women use that power is up to each individual. Women who have not stepped into their beauty, still carry emotional scars in the collective archetype that cover an inner emptiness they try to fill with a variety of addictions, self-sabotage and unequal relationships. This includes comfort eating, beauty products, alcohol, lovers and things to substitute their soul desire for intimacy. Even pain can fill the void by holding onto reasons for that *hurt* to exist by telling themselves stories they learn to believe through mere repetition. Some women seem unable to break out of the spider webs of their own design. The only way out of habitual patterns comes from the ability to see those patterns, from above or below the old beliefs that keep those disempowering stories in place.

So before you judge them, love them. You both want the same thing, you just have different ways of expressing it. The more love you can hold in your heart while your partner is going inwards, the less she will project at you what she cannot deal with inside. Anything can trigger her and you cannot fix it. But you can choose to be present.

Feminine expression needs a masculine witness
When women attempt to express their frustration from feeling used, they are ignored because it is seen as subjective. Society doesn't acknowledge their stories and they start to believe that the problem exists only in their minds. Society doesn't have accepted role model stories for what is felt by many women, and their feelings are not being validated. Misunderstood, they feel invisible and without value.

Beauty is truth and our ability to express it.
Beauty is felt when the masculine gaze accepts
the feminine's expression of the truth.

Feminine energy is opening like flowers all over, noticing each other, exhibiting radiance that wants to be noticed. With each collective feminine step, women invite the masculine to be their witness to transform into a radiant being. It is time for the truth to reveal her beauty. A new feminine is emerging, the likes of which society has not met, and she will not hide. The more she is discovering herself, the less she can be stopped from serving her role to change the consciousness of mankind.

As the shadow is healing in the female collective, beauty and radiance are becoming irresistible even to those who suppressed it. The feminine collective is claiming its power back. People are acting from right action more and more, and needing approval less and less. Each time one woman evolves into her natural beauty, she does it for all of humankind and promotes equality for both genders. One gender is not superior to another. Each one has a part to play in the new level of consciousness we are entering.

The presence of inner feminine beauty

Real beauty is a presence that surpasses understanding and explanation, and allows feelings of inclusion and complete acceptance. Every woman is called by her own soul to answer to the claim for her inner beauty and truth. Answering this call is what invites her to change her inner beauty routine and makes it equal to the outer reflection of herself. It asks her to align the purity of her intentions with the impeccability of her actions. Who doesn't want such a virtuous woman?

There are still men who feed pearls to pigs and communities that take her womanhood from her by cutting off her breasts. But we are working towards a tipping point in mass consciousness that will change what society will allow, like the man who takes her power through ignorance when she offers it, as she exposes her vulnerability. She will no longer allow this.

When nothing else can effect change, the strength of a soft woman can, which is why women may have to go *there* first.

The most powerful man knows the heart of a soft, sensual woman and if he doesn't share his bed with one, he has not lived.

History taught women to hide beauty

In truth, beauty has come with a price. In the eleventh century in China, there lived a Taoist woman named Sun Pu-erh who sought the path of enlightenment. She dedicated her life to truth, which caused her to seek out one of the great masters of enlightenment in her time. She hoped that he would take her as his student, which was the tradition.

The master soon came to recognise her passion and perseverance, and told Sun Pu-erh that if she truly wished to attain immortality she would need to travel to Loyang where she could cultivate the Tao. When Sun Pu-erh revealed her face to her master, he was taken aback by her beauty and told her that beauty would remain an obstacle to her enlightenment. He denied her permission to travel to Loyang for he believed that she would be the constant target for men wishing to overpower her and take advantage of her.

Unwilling to let her appearance be an obstacle to her path, she immediately went home to the kitchen to heat a wok full of cooking oil. When the oil began to boil Sun Pu-erh picked up the wok, closed her eyes, and poured it over her face. With scars etched across her skin, Sun Pu-erh returned to the master who, amazed by her sacrifice, gave her permission to travel to Loyang.

Our own perception of our beauty is either our greatest value or our greatest obstacle. By integrating who we are and understanding that external beauty is but a reflection of the soul, women will stop expecting their partners to do for them what they cannot do for themselves, which is to see themselves as beautiful. The effort that goes into creating external beauty can never substitute the inner desire of the soul to see itself as beautiful through another's eyes.

When a woman feels beautiful she radiates beauty outwards and that confidence is recognised by every man she meets as she reflects his own beauty back to him.

The greatest gift you can give your conscious partner is to see her as beautiful.

Inner beauty is being truthful and honest with yourself first and foremost. The truth is always beautiful even when it's ugly.

What is the feminine without the masculine?

Women don't see themselves as broken things that need fixing. Feelings are dynamic, although you might experience women as changing their minds constantly. It is easy for a woman to experience a man's focus as forceful and be alarmed by it. The roles of males and females need to change in terms of what a woman expects from the male role, and vice versa, as she reintegrates her shadow. If our relationships are to become equal and maintain their attraction, we need to be able to fulfil our own needs from the inside, and we will appreciate what the male has to offer, as well as value our own contributions. Conscious relationships reflect who we are, what parts we need to accept and stop rejecting, as well as teach us about love and how wonderful we already are. To be completely free in relationships we allow each other freedom of choice to be who we are already. We meet our own needs and don't ask anything from our partner that we aren't willing to do for ourselves. If you're asked to do something and you don't feel free to say no, then say no to create that freedom. Instead of changing your partner, search for the part of you that is reacting emotionally and accept the part of you that still fears not being accepted.

There is a new feminine role emerging and it cannot exist without the masculine.

Whether you choose to engage with it or try to suppress it, I believe we are reaching a tipping point in consciousness that will change gender roles inside relationships and our environments accordingly. Our need for beauty can finally find its place in our hearts, instead of on our faces. Beauty will affect everyone who gazes upon its radiance, contagiously. And the time has come to claim our beauty as we see ourselves as beautiful, not because we deserve it, but because we believe it. And now it is your turn: what is your masculine voice contributing to this dialogue?

True to feminine expression, I am leaving the discussion open here ... for you to continue the conversation.

Conclusion

As a man reading this you might feel the need for some conclusion. You might have been surprised at how emotional women are in their releasing expressions and wonder why you should yet again hear what a woman has to say, as I have shared some of my innermost thoughts. You might have felt your heart opening once or twice as you listened, or become aware of your own need to express for the masculine voice. You might feel anger at what is referred to as the feminine need and may even view them as projections. Women don't have the same need to draw conclusions or act on what is said; the art of expression heals us. It is how you feel when you express that heals you. Masculine energy extends outward in a focussed way and feminine energy draws in to embrace and nurture lovingly. Once we have expressed, it is easier to be open and be intimate and sensual. When the feminine steps into her power and leads with presence, she integrates both her inner masculine and feminine.

I realised while writing this book that devotion in a relationship is relevant to independent needs. When the feminine voice expresses, it is only respectful to allow the masculine to express their anger too, both internally and in the external relationship.

Our conditioning taught us that girls are objects of beauty and men are strong by manipulating their environment. But if a man leads from a place of confidence that is linked to societal values or related to money to give him power, a strong feminine woman can invite him into a respectful and balanced conscious relationship where they make their own rules and roles. You need to move out of a personal space of self-protection and stay soft and open if you are ever going to share equality and devotion to your partner without exploitation. As I realised this, the universe presented me with an example: my partner and I had a deep conversation. I talked about a deep personal struggle, seeking a solution. Sitting on the patio soaking up the winter sunlight, my partner did everything right as he stayed mentally present, except that his sunglasses were hiding his eyes. I needed to see his eyes to feel his mental presence and it was as if not seeing his eyes left me feeling disconnected. I asked him to remove his shades, which conflicted with his personal need to deal with the glare of the sun. His reaction was to be irritated, telling me that I was unreasonable. Doing so was serving his needs at the expense of mine. I acknowledged this and explained to him that I needed his support to go deep inside me to find my answer. I asked if it would be possible for him to demonstrate his devotion and love for the sake of the relationship. This could be a simple power struggle of choosing whose needs are more important. His devotion to us supported me to shift beyond my obstacles to find the hope that I needed to find the right action.

Relationships move through three stages: when my first husband died I was scared of being dependent on a man again, which highlights the risk of codependence. My partnership with my second husband lacked intimacy, because I was so focussed on independence. There was no shortage of physical connection; I am referring to an emotional and spiritual connection on a very open and intimate level. It is quite possible to experience physical chemistry and exclude the emotional, mental and spiritual connections that offer true connection and transparency on all levels in all three stages of the relationship. With my third life partner I realised that devotion shows unconditional love through love languages that take me from committing to a mechanical contract and covenant into a heart space of knowing that I love him because my heart is really in it. This doesn't mean my heart wasn't in it before when I started my relationships, but this time I was conscious of the implications of the type of commitment I made and at which levels I choose to connect with my partner. Devotion is what determines how the relationship plays out. If I choose to live with expectations of what I want from my partner in a co-dependence or serving all my needs independently and I don't grow into the next conscious stage, I will lose out on the potential for sharing. What I need to develop is devotion. What it will bring me is the support of sharing with my partner to live a life of respect and awe for each other, beyond expecting my partner to make me happy. Together we can co-create a new sacred space beyond feeling rejection and aloneness as we learn who we really are.

What if, by the end of this book, we understand that what happens inside the relationship is to open individual hearts? The need to understand each other is what drives the behaviour that repeatedly opens us and keeps us connected to that little soft voice inside us.

Each time we feel challenged, we can engage with the opportunity to understand the moral lesson behind the situation in our relationship. Know that life recreates the same pattern and the same set of circumstances, to invite you to take up the challenge to focus beyond the distractions that clutter your mind and heart, and that prevent you from hearing the soft inner voice of the soul. Our power to create lies in the focus we choose, the meanings we make in our minds and what we do about it. Finding the purpose in the *messages* through your relationship happens as you stay engaged, and learn through reflection who you really are as you accept more of yourself.

As long as we experience life as victims in our relationships, we have not yet learned to focus beyond our expectations on what is positive. The focus that allows hopeful perspectives leads us to act beyond the apparent obstacles in ways that pull us out of the challenge into the hero's journey. What we focus on determines whether we eventually act on the little voice inside us. When we experience the environment with a positive focus, our perspective brings hope that allows us to change our behaviour despite the obstacles. When we hear and act on the inner voice we inspire others with our actions. The key here is not just the focus, but the meaning we make of the changes as they happen. What we think about the value of ourselves when changes happen, and if we now also adjust our beliefs, will determine if we can keep the change.

When we are left with hope, our newly inspired actions empower us. If the new meaning we make of ourselves boosts our self-image and our ego becomes self-promoting (thinking how great we are) we miss the message of the inner voice, which is a humble one. When we can see our partner (or others) as reflections of who we are, the service to self for independent needs transforms into devotion to our partner. Our very selfless actions then become what keep us connected to that inner voice of God whispering to us through our partners. And those are the moments we start to understand that we are not separate from our partners, nor are they the enemy. We learn that even through mechanical giving, as they ask for their love language, at some point we might ask if our hearts are in it. Devotion teaches us to learn to give even when our partner rejects it, because we really get that we give to ourselves. We live with hope that the space we hold for them will bring the internal realisation that giving love is the lesson, like we would give it to ourselves. As love, we create more of ourselves by giving love. This is our nature. We get a glimpse of what respect for others (and ourselves) is and understand the universe as an interrelated expression of God Source. We might wonder, what if God is my wife? Conscious relationships start with awareness. But that is only the beginning. Conscious relationships also require new mental maps and theories, which become your own meanings through your values and beliefs. At this stage, only you can know what conscious relationship means to you. But all that means nothing unless you put it into practice.

I hope that sharing my insights will make a difference to men asking questions about understanding their partners. As a coach, I realised that many women I work with had not found their voices yet. Writing this book from my own journey perspective gave me a voice, and hopefully it will give a voice to the women who don't know how to express what they feel yet.

What does it all mean if no man accepts the challenge to build a new kind of supportive relationship where love and respect are considered before he acts on his own needs? Not all women are able to reconnect with their soft side when you see them as the enemy. So I dare you to act on your own inner voice and accept the invitation of your inner voice to become soft inside as you embrace your inner feminine. To hear the soft voice you have to *become* soft. See your partner as a reflection of God, and if you cannot do that ... a reflection of yourself. Everything as you know it today might change forever if you let it.

It takes courage to read a book like this. Keep it, and at times use the reference guide at the back to integrate more as you feel the need.

Recommended Reading & Bibliography

Bly, R. & Woodman, M. (1998). *The Maiden King*. Dorset: Element Books Ltd.

Deida, D. (1995). *Intimate Communion: Awakening Your Sexual Essence*. Florida: Health Communications Inc.

Deida, D. (1997). *The Way of the Superior Man*. Austin: Plexus.

Diener, E. & Biswas-Diener, R. (2008). *Happiness: Unlocking the Mysteries of Psychological Wealth*. Oxford: Blackwell Publishing.

Laslo, E. (2009). *The Akashic Experience*. Vermont: Inner Traditions.

Moore, T. (2004). *Dark Nights of the Soul*. London: Piatkus Books.

Moore, T. (1992). *Care of the Soul*. London: Piatkus Books.

Osho (2001). *Intimacy: Trusting Oneself and the Other*. New York: St Martin's Griffen.

Ruiz, M. (1997) *The Four Agreements: A Practical Guide to Personal Freedom*. California: Amber-Allen Publishing.

Sheldrake, R. (1981). *A New Science of Life*. London: Icon Books.

Villoldo, A. (2010). *Illumination*. US: Hay House, Inc.

Whitfield, C.L. (1987). *Healing the Child Within*. Florida: Health Communications Inc.

Zukav, G. (2010). *Spiritual Partnerships: The Journey to Authentic Power*. UK: Rider.

Index

A clear reflection, p.55
A longing to share, p.51
A map for appreciation, p.178
A partner who is ready, p.54
A woman opens when she feels beautiful, p.27
Accept your shadow, p.154
Acknowledging value keeps equality in place, p.72
Allow signs of not good enough to heal your stuff, p.117
Anatomy of emotions, p.232
Anger masks inner acceptance, p.206
Any need to defend yourself means you're not dealing with your stuff, p.83
Arm yourself with confidence, p.26
Ask her what her contribution is, p.278
Assist her to recognise her natural skills, p.262
Assist her to understand how tangible her value is, p.264
Attachments bounce off safe boundaries, p.132
Attitude determines a positive outlook, p.93
Be conscious of accountability, p.153

Be easy on yourself – unpack the facts from the emotion, p.258
Blame signifies the lack of responsibility for our role participation, p.272
Blaming is a signal that it is your stuff, p.83
Breaking commitments, p.64
Breakthroughs need vulnerability from her, p.106
Challenges have a meaningful sequence, p.205
Choose your focus: Energy flows where attention goes, p.92
Choosing a partner who reflects love to us, p.43
Choosing the inner feminine to lead her, p.230
Codependent relationships are not natural bonding, p.74
Conflict is a way of communicating to grow, p.256
Conflict is safe within boundaries, p.253
Conflict rules of engagement for respect, trust and equality, p.255
Create internal feedback resources, p.153
Creating closeness consciously and safely, p.145

Cutting cords of attachment strengthens conscious relationships, p.135
Dealing with her own mother, p.244
Deciding if we are good enough comes from the ego's need for purpose, p.113
Differentiate between self-love and being a victim, p.242
Does love bring two people together, p.37
Don't mistake being alone for rejection, p.126
Do you ever feel she is testing you?, p.229
Drawing wisdom from knowledge, p.91
Each rejection creates a feeling of separation anxiety at first, p.124
Emotions are the alarm bells warning us that we have stuff to deal with, p.85
Encourage her emotional intelligence, p.262
Encourage her to express her value, p.281
Encourage her to take her power back, p.175
Equality avoids games, p.53
Every action has a positive intention if we can find it, p.85
Every breakthrough requires that we learn a spiritual lesson, p.96
Every part reflected at you that you deny is your stuff, p.84
Every time we feel lonely we can accept more of the love we are, p.124
Express honestly, p.54
Express needs and be prepared to fulfil them yourself, p.72
Fears are empty when we look at them directly, p.187
Feeling the pain, p.231
Feminine energy is like glue for diversity and potential conflict, p.263
Feminine expression needs a masculine witness, p.287
Finding her way to inner appreciation, p.174

Finding ourselves again by searching for God, p.122
For her to be vulnerable she needs to feel safe, p.108
Forgiveness, p.87
Freedom allows a new game of co-creation, p.155
Freedom means we don't judge, p.152
Get energy from your inner source rather than through exchanging energy, p.135
Give her power back to enhance intimacy, p.277
Give the feminine a real voice, p.286
Giving the feminine boundaries, p.229
Giving without expecting something releases attachment, p.132
Has she accepted her nature to nurture? p.173
Healing your insecurity, p.29
Her feminine leadership skills will be her advantage, p.264
History of structure and flow development, becoming one, p.270
History taught women to hide beauty, p.288
Hope doesn't give up, p.102
How can we bring intimacy back into gender roles? p.269
How does she give? Is she generous or greedy? p.208
How much honesty is too much?, p.141
How much talking is necessary?, p.142
How she learns about her beauty, p.175
How to appreciate the ultimate woman, p.179
How we give permission for attachment, p.133
If you don't know who you are, learned rules can divide you, p.81
Ignorance of the inner connection, p.222
Integrity of doing, p.57
Internal resistance expresses outward as conflict, p.257

Intimacy provides the closest reflections, p.143
Introducing the value of a spiritual understanding, p.95
Intuition teaches us how much closeness we need, p.144
Is she lazy or courageous? p.212
Is there enough love to grow together?, p.39
It's easier for you to see her stuff than it is for her, p.105
It is human nature to avoid pain and seek pleasure, p.226
It takes two people to make a commitment, p.67
Keep a space for faith, p.180
Know thyself, p.52
Knowing ourselves is the foundation for freedom, p.152
Leading as the new feminine, p.200
Learning freedom from ancient wisdom, p.152
Listening invites close reflection, p.143
Live with spiritual integrity, p.155
Looking into the mirror, p.32
Love reflects how integrated we are, p.40
Love yourself to free yourself from neediness, p.153
Making love can be an expression of intimacy, p.160
Making way for the emerging feminine, p.286
Many healthy ways to connect, p.74
Most things are relative; Perspective is everything, p.43
Moving deeper into the feminine: Getting to know ourselves, p.228
Mutual respect for values, p.56
Name the attachment to bring it out of hiding, p.132
Nurturing does not mean being in control, p.249
Nurturing pain, p.249

Nurturing requires emotional sensitivity, p.243
Observation changes everything, p.109
Opening a woman for sexual intimacy, p.167
Our nature is to be free to love, p.165
Overcoming jealousy, p.214
Overindulgence or wisdom, p.216
Pain closes women, p.25
Penetrate her with your focus, p.27
Polarity sets the stage for intimacy, p.275
Pride, p.216
Projecting is your stuff, p.82
Projection, p.33
Recognising her closed heart, p.177
Recognising love, p.46
Recognising the feminine, p.226
Rejecting parts of ourselves, p.221
Rejection teaches us to love ourselves more, p.246
Relationship is a conscious choice, p.41
Relationships are mirrors we look into to see our stuff, p.85
Replace attachment with conscious bonding, p.134
Respect for each other allows us to connect freely, p.161
Responsibility to deal with your own stuff, p.54
Rigid, defined roles kill our freedom, p.268
Rock bottom is where it's at, p.103
Saying "I love you", p.44
Seeking common values, p.269
Sensuality is natural for a woman who feels beautiful, p.273
Share to connect for freedom, p.146
Sharing of beingness and understanding lessons, p.56
She focuses first on relationships, p.180
Speaking for closeness, p.142
Stages of transformation, p.193
Substitute lust for closeness, p.210
Symbolic meaning of the dragonfly, p.194

Take responsibility for your own happiness to be free, p.151
Take responsibility for your own happiness, p.52
Take time out rather than pretend to listen, p.186
Taking responsibility for what is ours, p.97
Taking responsibility provides a platform for equality, p.72
The accountability to be physically intimate, p.162
The biological triggers in the female body, p.196
The desire to connect intimately for women, p.163
The emerging feminine, p.197
The emerging masculine, p.198
The first understanding of feeling separate, p.121
The inability to hear comes from the pain of shutting down, p.186
The influence of conditioned learning, p.222
The masculine gift to the feminine, p.168
The need for appreciation is a soul desire, p.177
The philosophical perspective of inner masculine and feminine, p.196
The power to connect intimately comes from pure essence, p.163
The presence of inner feminine beauty, p.288
The previously suppressed feminine, p.200
The public persona of the developing feminine, p.199
The purpose of symbolic events, p.204
The real purpose of attachment is to imprison our minds from observing all that is there, p.137
There are times when good communication cannot fix a relationship but calibrating values can, p.73
The rejected self is the shadow, p.39
The responsibilities you commit to, p.63
The value of patience in breaking through, p.101
The wall of not sharing pushes us away, p.144
The work of love, p.45
There is an inner knowing, p.63
To know if it is your stuff you need to know yourself, p.80
To receive appreciation one needs to be able to appreciate one's self first, p.178
Transferring bonding from family to partner, p.122
Trust life to teach you freedom, p.155
Trust your partner, responsibly, where your values do not overlap, p.269
Two people connect intimately to invite a higher presence, p.159
Understanding her own needs through projection, p.174
Understanding rules in conscious relationships, p.79
Understanding the dynamic of polarity to create growth, p.271
Unlearning conditioned behaviour: Revealing the inner feminine, p.224
Unlearning conditioned projections, p.227
Values and beliefs create perspective, p.94
Vulnerability is powerful when it is authentic, p.280
We feel love when we pull our projections back, p.41
We keep repeating the same experiences until we learn from them, p.248
We nurture what we value, p.244
We value what we can accept, p.245
What does she really want from sharing with a partner she can trust? p.279
What have people said about her in the past that touched her, true or not? p.279
What is feminine leadership? p.261

What is intimacy? p. 267
What is the feminine without the masculine? p.289
What we try so hard to avoid is where we find the answers we seek, p.188
What you can expect to get from a commitment, p.64
What you commit to, p.62
What you need to make a commitment, p.62
When it's not your stuff you still have a role to play, p.86
When we cannot break through, p.98
Who you are is enough, p.116

Why we need to understand attachments in relationships, p.133
Witnessing with love heals, p.188
Women increase human capital and shift perspectives, p.263
Women make great managers, p.263
You are the power of her beauty, p.276
You may not be able to save her – only she can save herself, p.190
Your confidence reflects her beauty, p.28
Your partner's role when experiencing stuckness, p.95
Your role as partner is to witness, p.103

Author Biography

Adelé Green is a sentient being and a freelance writer. She is published in the NY bestseller series Thank God I 'Empowered Women'. She is a qualified Coach and Kinesiologist who has been in private practice since 2007 in Johannesburg, South Africa. She is also a thought leader in transformation and has designed and implemented programmes for women and gender mainstreaming. She is equally skilled in writing poetry and fire walking.

For more information about products by the author, go to www.nakedwithadele.com

Lightning Source UK Ltd.
Milton Keynes UK
UKHW020453250419
341590UK00010B/1030/P